D0325827

LIZARDS EAT BUTTERFLIES

"*Do—not unto, but with—others.* As elegantly as possible—not to someone else's standard." Lizards Eat Butterflies transforms the way you look at the world. I learned to consider more and judge less. It re-framed many of my beliefs. It enabled me to actually Fully Live. I am deeply grateful for this guide back to our humanity.

— **Amanda Gore**
globally renown public speaker

WARNING: In order to decipher this masterpiece, you will require a dictionary, Google, a tub of Ben & Jerry's and an open mind.

—**Philip Højgaard-Olsen**
Muscular Dystrophy Global Advocate

F#%* Yeah! What if the world really counted on you?
Live in it. Love it. And don't seek to fly away! We all need US!

—**David Cutler**
EatMedia Founder

Lizards Eat Butterflies

An Antidote to the Self-Help Addiction

News Flash! *The world doesn't revolve around you.* **You are not the, or even a, point**. *You are a temporary arrangement of matter and energy that is inextricably part of the fabric of everything and as such, your mission, should you choose to accept it, is to make your best con-tribution regardless of the challenges, the frustrations, the pains or the joys. Do—not unto—but with others. As elegantly as possible —not to someone else's standard. And celebrate the propagation of your goodness and elegance rather than expecting it to bounce back to you. Far from the Golden Rule —this is the Lightness of Life!*

Contents

Lights

I received a phone call from Robert Prinable as he was in the midst of his cancer treatment in Thailand.

"David," he stated, his voice conveying the exhaustion he felt, "I think I'm going to die soon."

"That's great!" I replied in a proportionally inappropriate tone.

"You're the worst friend a guy could have. What makes it great?" he probed.

"Well," I began, "at your 70th birthday party, I got to meet so many of your amazing friends and had such a great time that I figure even more cool people will show up for your funeral."

Robert laughed, his spirits obviously lifting from the sullen swamp into which they had tumbled.

"Plus," I continued, "we haven't finished our book."

"Book?" he snapped. "I didn't know we were writing a book."

"That's because we haven't started it yet," I responded.

"So what are we writing?" he mused, taking the bait.

"We're going to update Plato's *Republic* in a modern conversation," I responded.

"That's a great idea. Let's start when I get back from Thailand."

Each weekend until two weeks before his passing, Robert and I would engage in conversations—sometimes just the two of us and sometimes with Bernadette (Robert's wife) and Kim (my wife)—regarding the essence of living. These conversations were witnessed, at times, by Sarah Hatcher (who transcribed the recorded ones), Shanti Clements, and Peter Hojgaard-Olsen all who added their perspectives into the dialogue Robert and I shared. Sitting around the dining room table on 4 June

1

2017 in Fairlight NSW overlooking the Manly coast, we finished Robert's work. His book, and life, came to a close. And my task began.

I could say that I started writing this book on the 12th of November 2017 as I crossed the Equator on United 99 from Melbourne to Los Angeles. In truth, I waited to start writing until I had found a peace of mind for which I had been waiting my entire life. Kim Martin—the consummate partner for fully living—has created a space in my being that allows my thoughts to focus on life rather than rationalizing my attempts to survive. My gratitude to Kim is overwhelming. For it is her persistent evidence of living with gratitude in each present moment that has showed me that the *Subtle Art of Being Human* is not an ephemeral ideal. It is fully accessible. Robert tasted this in the moments before his passing and I've been blessed to drink deeply from the river of life that bathes the soul and no longer seeks anything.

This book represents a lifetime of perspectives. The warp upon which I will weave this tapestry is gratitude. And it is only fitting that I acknowledge those without whom this book would not exist. The Gratitude Arc of this book starts with the funeral of my Grandpa Martin in 1976. At his funeral at New Holland Mennonite Church I remember sitting in the pew singing one of his favorite hymns, *My Jesus, I Love Thee*. That was the day it hit me. Through the sultry harmonies of hymns, I was being brain-washed. "For thee all the follies of sin I resign." In four-part harmony, it sounds so innocuous. But I was sitting with hundreds of others at the funeral of a man who never fully lived so one day he could have his reward "in heaven"! "I love thee for thou hast first loved me." Really? How on Earth could I justify what life had dealt me with an abstract illusion entitled to my love for an illusion I was told was true? As I dropped a rose on his lowered casket as it entered the farmland that had sustained the Martin family in Pennsylvania since the early 1700s, I knew I would never fit the box. Robert and I spoke of this enculturated epistemological trap many times. Recite that you're a sinner. Recite that something unverifiably "out there" is the adjudicator of "right" and "wrong" and represents an aspirational ideal beyond mortal access and, voila, you've denigrated humanity to servitude!

That funeral vaulted our family from California to Pennsylvania where I spent the next 8 years of my life with the glorious exception of a summer in Arkansas. I'm grateful for the dozens of churches that littered my adolescence—each insisting on their "truth" by diminishing humanity and the perspectives of others. I'm grateful for the relentless criticism of dogma, doctrine, and exposition that marked every Sunday, many Wednesday evenings and each night's devotions. Listening to the cacophony of "right" when none was in coherence gave me a chance to discern my path—a road far less traveled.

I'm grateful for my youthful arrogance that turned down the Presidential Scholarship to Lehigh Valley University in favor of Goshen College's global service idealism. And I'm grateful that I met Colleen in the Westlawn dorm in the Fall of 1985 and spent the next 30 years navigating a journey through life with her. I'm grateful that, on that journey, we moved to Virginia where I met the late Senator Emily Couric who channeled my foresight into legislative reform to celebrate the innovation of academics at the University of Virginia. I'm grateful that on this mission, I occasioned to meet Morgan Percy who then introduced me to John Petersen who put my foresight onto a global stage through The Arlington Institute.

And on a morning in Gold Coast, Australia, I'm grateful that Christine McDougall listened to a podcast that had been posted by Arlington Institute's Ken Dabkowski which set in motion the relationship that led to Todd Goldfarb. For it was Todd's recording of my thoughts in 2011 that found their way to Sydney where Robert, and his friend Peter Hojgaard-Olsen, tuned into *Worldwide Tipping Point* thinking they were going to hear Ken Wilber only to find my voice instead. And upon hearing my podcast, Peter and Robert sat together and wrote the note that animated Robert and my relationship.

Oh, and let's remember, but for Christine's relentless efforts to get *In-*

tegral Accounting discussed in Australia—a mission that became a shared one with Robert, Peter, Bernadette and many others—I wouldn't have met Julio De Laffitte and the *Unstoppables*; I wouldn't have gone to Antarctica; I wouldn't have been on Deception Island on 2 February 2015; and, I wouldn't have met the inestimable Kim Martin who is entirely responsible for affording me the confidence of being me, the luxury of being at peace, and the love that provides space for genuine contemplation.

This book contains the echoes of many conversations. And while some will go unmentioned, in addition to those already mentioned, I wish to acknowledge: Dustin DiPerna, Bob Kendall, Theresa Arek, Lorraine Mill, Jon Darrall-Rew, Amanda Gore, Leo Burke, Jan De Dood, Lisette Schuitemaker, Edward West, Pieter Fourie, David Pratt, my wonderful children, Katie and Zachary, and, most recently, Sienna, Elizabeth Lindsey, Michael Richardson-Borne, Tony Weller, Steve Trevino, Chip Duncan, Ken Wilber, Cyrus the Great, Frank Vitolo, Plato, Socrates, Pope Innocent III, Gregory Bateson, Buckminster Fuller, Karl Popper, the Council of Nicea, Sun Wukong, and Zoroaster. More importantly, I acknowledge every whisper, thought and echo from all those who have unleashed their certitude about the capacity of humanity whose names and likenesses have been erased in the inertial friction of dominant, repressive social order. Your form and identity may have been forgotten but, as matter and energy cannot be created or destroyed, I acknowledge that the thoughts and perspectives herein are not "mine". I merely had, in a moment, the opportunity to synthesize the Wisdom held by so many to slow them into written form.

Lizards Eat Butterflies follows the structure of Plato's *Republic* by design. While much of modernity seeks to idealize the Greek philosopher's discourse, the animating context for Plato's work is seldom critiqued. As Robert and I discussed this, we became increasingly aware of the insidious consequence of this callous assent to the unconsidered milieu for the *Republic*. The Greek conversation was devoid of explicit critiques on what it meant to be fully human.

The book you're holding has been considered. After the first draft was written, I had the honor of reading it to Amanda Gore, Lorraine Mill, and Kim. After that first pass, it was edited and critiqued by Nicolas Wales, Amanda Gore (several times), Sarah Hatcher, Dustin DiPerna, Kerry Dugan, Natalia Rose, Sacha Stone, Philip Olsen, Art Murray, David Cutler, William Wismann, Bruce Wright, Dan Goldstein, Kenny Polcari, Edward West, Sandi Brown, Christian Nagle, and Qianfan Wu.

While the lizard on the cover represents the tangible work of my beautiful wife Kim Martin, the entirety of this book is a tribute to her life and love. In all my writings before this book, I struggled to overcome the dissonance of knowing that I was propping up an illusion in my life. With patience and love, Kim has made a home from which I can contemplate, consider, and communicate what deeply matters to me and share it with you. Her passion for exploring human potential—what it means to *Fully Live*—has become our shared vision. For her resolute confidence, tireless encouragement, Spartan bluntness, and passionate love, I'm eternally grateful.

Lizards Eat Butterflies

Treachery.

There are millions of untold stories echo-
ing in the Cave in which
elegance, beauty, and mercy narrate the march of days.

But these stories are untold, and thus, treachery prevails.

This is one untold story.
Told by a witness to a world in which
Persistent, Generative, and Infinitely Orthogonal
Humanity flourishes in full Transparency.

A gift of Love to:
Katie, Zachary, Sienna,
Amanda, Nic, and Lorraine...,
and most of all,
Kim

Camera

Michael asked me for my ID as he was preparing my security pass to enter the New York Stock Exchange trading floor a few years ago. I reached into my pocket—this time it was buttoned—and pulled out my tattered brown leather wallet.

"Here you go," I said as I handed it over the desk at the Broad St. entrance just past the blue security tent.

"How've you been?" Michael asked in a Brooklyn accent straight from central casting.

"Great," I said swinging my backpack off my shoulder to get it ready for its passage through the scanner.

Just then, the door swung open allowing a waft of Manhattan's air into the conditioned foyer. A world-renowned, human potential, "spiritually enlightened", *transcendent*, celebrity entered. He was wearing black jeans, a gray shirt and was accessorized with trendy spectacles and sockless shoes. He's one of those guys who is advocating getting to a next level, "beyond human," state!

As he glided up to the security desk, Michael reflexively reminded him of the New York Stock Exchange's dress code.

"Sir," he began, "if you'd like to go onto the Stock Exchange floor, you're kindly requested to wear proper business attire."

"You must not know who I am," was the visitor's response.

"I'm sorry, Sir, but that's our policy," Michael calmly chided.

Before this situation could progress, a young woman appeared in the glass doorway on the left side of the desk, effusively greeted the visitor, and whisked him past the security guards.

"He's on air shortly," she said as the two of them disappeared into the marbled corridor.

Michael printed my badge, ushered me through security and welcomed me on the other side of the scanner.

"Thanks for being...well, I guess, normal," he said handing me my badge.

****

If you're super cool, spiritual, or enlightened (which I'm sure you are if you're reading this book), you've had about a million encounters with butterfly metaphors. Gurus, talk-show hosts, life coaches, greeting cards all extolling the wonder and magic of the lowly gluttonous caterpillar turning into a beautiful butterfly through the magic of "*imaginal cells.*"

If you're even more amazing and "present", you will dutifully inform others that you're going through some sort of chrysalis moments when you want to spiritualize your denial of a behavior, experience or relationship in which you've decided that it's someone or something else's fault.

Maybe you've eaten a few too many *Ben & Jerry's* while *processing* your grief—it's your caterpillar phase. Maybe you've decided that mouse-clicks and remote controls are strenuous enough and you just can't leave your *Netflix* series to get off the couch—it's larval baby. Maybe your discovery of plus sized activewear and bulky fleece has been your middle-finger to the patriarchy—pupal plush! Maybe you've treated people like shit but want to feign immaturity and your 'shadow' self—your delicate wings are emerging! Aahhh! Precious.

Sorry, that was a rough start. I didn't mean it was you. I meant it was that annoying friend that you have. You know the one? She always makes it about her. He is so desperate for attention that it's maddening. After all, you've *done the work*! You've watched some amazing TED talks on vulnerability, grief, and butterflies. You've cold pressed your celery juice while watching late morning television and have seen the umpteenth *next amazing guest* regurgitating the same oozy messages about metamorphosis while being relentlessly bombarded with ads for erectile dysfunction (for him—cuz it's not about her), anti-depressants (with suicidal thoughts as a leading side-effect), and life insurance (so your loved ones aren't screwed with the debt you've run up in life).

And of course, you've put on the few extra pounds. After all, your job is stressful, and you have to spend 45 minutes more in traffic because you're living in the suburbs. After the kids, you just don't have you time to stay fit like that annoying yoga instructor you see in the carpool line at school. Thank god someone came up with the caterpillar story to hold out hope for your emergent you.

On Earth Day in 1990, Norie Huddle released *Butterfly*. Maybe it was because it was Earth Day. Maybe it was because spiritual 'luminaries' such like Barbara Marx Hubbard, Deepak Chopra, Eckhart Tolle, Oprah Winfrey and the Alliance for The New Humanity took to Huddle's story like fruit flies to ripe bananas. WTF! Fruit flies? No, David, we're talking about butterflies! We love butterflies. They're pretty. They make us feel light, yet vulnerable—fragile, yet dreamy.

Oh shit. That's the problem. If only Jan Swammerdam, the 17th century Dutch biologist who first observed the imaginal discs which serve to form the physiological template for metamorphosis had done his work on butterflies! What a shame that Norie bastardized these fruit fly-inspired actual structures into positivism ripe for misappropriation and distraction when she popularized the term "imaginal cells" in butterflies. "Imaginal" in biology didn't mean "imagination" or some sort of wistful longing—it meant "template". Lost in translation lead to abject positivist embezzlement. Unfortunately for Swammerdam—and for the whole of humanity that suffered for over 310 years without an Oprah Winfrey show or a Deepak Chopra lecture—he and the rest of the scientific community studied fruit flies and fruit flies are annoying pests.

Spinning imaginal discs first identified in fruit fly pests into butterfly bullshit was just what the world was missing to complete the philosophy of self-absorption that has flooded bookstores and airwaves for the past 40 years. Introducing the flighty, whimsical butterfly metamorphosis (or more correctly, holometabolism) into pop pseudo-science finished the butterfly myth that desperately needed individualism to get it landed in the power of positivism.

After all, for three decades, "The Butterfly Effect", a term coined by MIT mathematician Edward Lorenz in the early 1960s[1], was being mis-appropriated by human potentiality advocates as the justification for all manner of empty heroic transformation narratives. Unwilling to embrace our callous neglect for ourselves, our actions, or our environment, we prefer making up a story about how there's a 'better' 'tomorrow' or that somehow lemonade will come from the lemons. We defer accountability by kicking our complicity into an anonymous happy ending.

For new players, the Butterfly Effect was the notion that in chaotic and complex systems, a single and small perturbation in one place can unleash disproportionately gargantuan effects in another system. Famously, "A butterfly flaps its wings in the Amazonian jungle, and subsequently a storm ravages half of Europe."[2]

Those who felt that positive thinking or spirituality would solve the *big problems* loved the Butterfly Effect. It felt good to associate with a butterfly. After all, what's not to like about its ethereal beauty?

But unfortunately, Lorenz's effect (and math) actually shows that almost EVERY ACTION is meaningless and that there's no way on God's Green Earth to ever predict which single, improbable act will have any effect.

Worse still, Lorenz was clear that the flapping of the wing was as likely to be destructive as constructive. So, it's pretty dubious for us to decide we want to flap when our flapping is equally likely to do nothing, unleash Armageddon, or send a happy face emoji to a friend in need.

But like all other psychobabble positivity, selling opiates of self-absorption and *empowerment* is the very drug our irrelevant social apathy gobbles up…kind of like a voracious caterpillar as it gorges itself prior to dissolving into a gooey mess in its chrysalis.

1. Edward Lorenz. "Deterministic Nonperiodic Flow." *Journal of the Atmospheric Sciences.* Vol.20, pp 130-141, March 1963.
2. Terry Pratchett & Neil Gaiman, *Good Omens: The Nice and Accurate Prophecies of Agnes Nutter, Witch.* William Morrow, United Kingdom. 1990.

Put the efficacy of the Butterfly Effect in collective unconsciousness. Add the fairy tale that within each of us—in our imaginal cells—is a pretty, pretty princess or prince and, voila, you get millions of viewers, you have books fly off shelves, and you have book clubs and reading circles into which you can sell more Spandex and fad diets than you can shake a stick at. And while the whole butterfly thing feels like it should feel good, somewhere along the line, the dysfunction that plagues most of our lives and actual experiences feels like we're being sold a myth. Norie's Earth Day flapping unleashed a tsunami of breathless moments of meaninglessness in the form of millions of pages of self-help books and thousands of hours of TV claptrap.

That part worked. But since Earth Day 1990, we've slashed forests, burnt millions of hectares of our world, paved farmland, toxified water and air, blindly ignored the mining of minerals necessary for our iPhones unleashing the massacre of millions all while euthanizing our conscience by 'believing' that our chrysalis of indifference and gluttony will give way to a beautiful butterfly. Well here's some reality. We're not emerging, we don't have pretty wings, and our pretense of concern for love and spirituality has barely hidden our naked neglect of the world, its resources and its inhabitants…including us.

Lizards eat butterflies. Lizards also eat fruit flies. There are a lot of lizards. In fact, just maybe you're a lizard just like me.

Think about it. Lizards are pretty cool. They're basically small dinosaurs. They're the only creatures we observe that seem to defy gravity despite being big enough that it shouldn't work. Lizards appear to have no obstacles. If they see a wall—climb it. If they see a ceiling—just run upside down. Water—no worries—just spread your toes and run. *Wouldn't it be amazing to see the world with the 'can do' spirit of the lizard?*

Check it out. Like a bunch of other animals (you included, you big skin sack!) when their skin doesn't fit, they go through a mangy phase called molting and emerge all shiny and sleek. They don't pretend to *be* something that they weren't before (no worm turning into lilting butterfly). Instead, when one phase ends, they shed the skin that no longer serves, scrape the old, dead skin off, and emerge as themselves... just bigger and shinier. They're fast, sporty, ubiquitous (they live on every continent on Earth except Antarctica), and they out-run, out-live, and out-smart most of the rest of the animal kingdom.

Romans and Greeks carved them into stones. Chinese, Indians, Africans and Americans made them part of the hieroglyphic record. You'd be hard pressed to find any place where some kid isn't playing with a lizard at any point in time. Heck, they're probably more transiently loved by children than dogs and cats. In short, lizards are awesome. Oh, and they eat butterflies.

So, what's my gripe with butterfly stories? Well, thanks for asking. Like lizards, butterflies have been estimated to arrive on the scene roughly 200 million years ago (if you want to take stock in the dating of the fossil record). Like lizards, they go through a crawly phase. Like lizards, they occupy every continent except Antarctica. Like lizards, while they're caterpillars, they can crawl on or up nearly anything. Like lizards, they've fascinated cultures ranging from Egypt to Ecuador for thousands of years.

So far, things are looking pretty good. But my problem is this. Holometabolism or metamorphosis is misconstrued to infer that beings change and as a result, is a seductive message to tell a bloated and apathetic populace who would rather passively listen to televised bullshit than get off their ass and make a difference. And yes, I'm being blunt. And no, I don't mind if it's offensive. Because if this offends you, you're my audience.

The fact of the matter is, whether it's the fruit fly or butterfly, metamorphosis is about gluttonous consumption—NOT about transformation. The egg—larva—pupae—adult cycle suspends a population in inaction until food is abundant. After the caterpillars' defoliating other species' leaves, fruit or stem, the cocoon or chrysalis is advanced digestion chamber from which emerges the week-long sexual orgy of winged beasts which, having mated, lay their eggs in devastating abundance to begin the process of gluttonous consumption all over again. And it's no surprise that the spiritual elite of our time have figured out gushing optimistic winged fantasy appeals to the gluttonous masses who would rather be "inspired" than actually DO anything.

What's the point of this book?

For the past 30 years, I've been working with people who are sure that they want to *change*. What this means is that they've determined that there's something about their life that is not the way they want it. However, in that same period, I've noticed that while the clarity around what isn't working seems to be universally clear, the ability to nominate a "better" condition devoid of comparison—in other words, what would "good" look like?—is absent. We seem to be adept in finding things in life, things about our experience or our environment that we're sure *should* be different.

I've never seen anyone aspire to embrace full responsibility for their own lived experience out of the gate. I've never met a person who has the audacity or humility to recognize, that as the judge and jury on what's wrong, the possibility exists that 'ideal' is not an elusive aspiration but rather the unconsidered fantasy of a life or condition yet unlived. *Put more bluntly, if life is shitty, there's a reasonable chance that a major contributing factor is you and your perception.* We hear that, "the grass is greener" but have you ever actually eaten grass? Green grass, dead grass, or dirt—none of them are very edible. Last time I checked, you're not a cow or goat.

So back to 'changing'. I've got some really tragic news. You're not going to. You *can* alter your perception. You *can* deepen your awareness. You *can* limit your reflexive responses and choose to live a more considered existence. But you change you? Not a chance. When your mother and father put in motion the cell division that became you—pause, think about that blessed moment and now come back—you incarnated as you are. And while the tangled tapestry of your chromosomes can glitch here or there resulting in varying expressions at the margins, in the main, you are exactly as you were architected.

You do not change.

Worse still, the pulse that beats within you, the cells that replicate and recycle around you, and the behaviors which reflexively emerge from your encounter with life are largely not your own. And as such, the notion that you enjoy the equanimity that would be required to correctly assess your current condition or even recognize one that you've never lived or considered is delusional.

For the most part, you don't know what you're looking for most of the time and as such wouldn't recognize 'good' if it bit you in the arse! The ego prerequisite to prop up the cult of 'change' suggests that you somehow can reboot or rewire yourself. I'm going to discuss, in the opening chapter, a thesis that suggests change is not only an illusion but more dramatically, it's a pathologic and metastatic condition that robs you of life.

Far from altering the organism or the conditioned behaviors thereof, modern spiritual "transformation", "change", "evolution", or "transcendence" passes judgment on the inadequacy of the present and defers accountability and stewardship for the field effects each of us animate. In other words, we rationalize that which we do not consider because taking responsibility for our actions is too much effort.

Like the beliefs that animated two millennia of Dark Ages-level mythological veneration of prophets and their bastardized dogma, our self-proclaimed 'post-modern' cults seek to leave behind that which they find mundane without recognizing that the virus of venal vicissitude travels within the very fabric of our enculturated existence. That which makes us uncomfortable we distance with pejorative platitudes never considering the cumulative impact of our neglect for ourselves and the invisible system upon which we depend. "We have met the enemy, and they are ours".[3]

If we called 'change' what it really is—a lazy supplication to escape that which seems too challenging to engage differently—we'd be less likely to seek it so publicly. If we truly owned that we'd rather a fairy tale of

3. Oliver Hazard Perry, American Naval Officer in the 1813 Battle of Lake Erie.

saccharin avoidance than the dance with the stinging bees to drink the real nectar of the Sun than we'd begin the journey from obese caterpillar to svelte lizard.

But that would mean that the secondary gains that we get from being the victims of unconsidered existence would fall away and we'd be left standing stark naked in front of the mirror looking at the entire source of our dissatisfaction. Alas, sitting on a couch listening to Sirens crooning their seduction song to fat caterpillars is so much more…um…well… let's not go there?

Let me geek out for a moment. Reflexes—those behaviors thought to be commonly shared by humans and lizards (and other reptiles)—*are stimulus dependent.* Something 'happens' and the organism is compelled to act. Reflex behavior largely takes place in the spinal cord, not in the cerebral (thinking) cortex. And while all of us can think about the doctor's hammer hitting our knee to make our leg jump or the hand recoiling from the hot stove, we don't spend much time mapping the actual activity of a reflex.

Let's keep it simple. I stub my left toe on a nail. Immediately, my hamstrings and glutes in my left leg pull my foot back. Good so far? That's the part we all see. Oh, and I might blurt out some sort of expletive. Sorry for that!

What we don't see is what else happened. The same stimulus that pulled my left leg back by activating my hamstrings and gluteals told my left quadriceps muscle to totally disengage, and…, and this is where it gets really tricky, told my right side to act in direct opposition to what happened in my left leg. My right quads fired to stabilize my body while my right hamstrings accommodated by relaxing. Simplified, a reflex achieves its 'desired' outcome by selectively *disengaging and reinforcing* what you don't see. Pretty cool that people and lizards share this anatomical reality, right?

Here's where the problem comes in. You might be really good at diagnosing a stimulus that you don't like. You hate how men treat women. You hate how the 1% keep getting richer while the bottom 50% get poorer. You hate how your partner looked at that person. You can't countenance how people are dumb enough to fall for political or social propaganda. You can't tolerate sin. You can't stand carnivores. You get the point?

Each of these, like a reflex hammer, stimulates a response. Protest, march, isolate, ostracize, repent, advocate—all reflexive behaviors to be free of odious impulses, right? WRONG. These behaviors, like all spinal reflexes, serve only to *disengage* conscious, considered action and *reinforce* the artificial social templates which enslave thought and considered conduct. We want freedom *from* without considering what is getting disengaged and reinforced with our reflexive, aversion energy.

And this, my friends, adds to my antipathy to self-help. Can we identify things we don't like? Probably, at a symptom level. But do we really take the time to figure out the underlying stimulus that triggers that distaste? Almost never. Worse still (take a look at the stimuli I described two paragraphs up), do we take time to consider a world where women and men truly reverenced each other's uniqueness; where we stopped pretending that wealth and hording money are synonymous; where erotic appreciation didn't mean infidelity but rather the celebration of natural beauty; where dialogue meant first fully embracing the context that gives rise to political or social ideology; where diversity takes precedence over projected deviance; and, where sustenance is about reverential energy exchange?

You see, self-help and change are about adjudicating 'better' from a perspective of 'worse'—seeing redemption through broken lenses. We're missing the narratives and the tools to consider the perfection of now and recognize that its perceived imperfections are most probably *our projection* of 'absent' from the present. We are addicted to the reflex of freedom never bathing in the fountains of liberty in which all is functioning in every moment in its perfection.

This book is for the lizards. The flight of foot. The doers. This book is for people who want to get deeply in touch with themselves, the stories that have robbed them of their most fulfilling existence and want to live the most rewarding life possible. This book is a means to decipher the stories that we've been told, the people who have benefited from our belief therein, and a not-so-subtle suggestion to send those stories and their purveyors packing. This is for those who have had it with butterflies and are ready to meet the world devoid of obstacles… and eat butterflies.

And now for the rather copious disclaimers. This is the most loving thing I could write. Coming from a person who despised the word "love" for most of my life, that's not saying much, now is it? What I mean is that I've come to understand that words that keep us ensnared in an unconsidered illusion are neither kind nor loving.

This is a *rip-the-bandage-off* kind of book. It's not meant to 'feel good'.

What it IS meant to do is help you really feel.

And that's not an easy or light proposition. I've elected a tone that many will find confronting. This is by design. I'm entirely fed up with the era of faux sensitivity which has watered down messages that must be delivered plainly. My explicit intent is to offend. Not to be a jerk. Rather, my aim is analogous to a physician wielding a reflex hammer. The goal is not a sadistic impulse to inflict pain. Instead it serves as a provocation to consider the root of the reflex.

Who told you to be offended? What story were they trapped in? Who was being served by your offended sensibilities? How many times did you wish you could "speak your mind" only to repress the impulse?

We live in an era of callous brutes. And before you think I'm referring to one gender—let me disabuse you of that notion. Yes, we have the 'grab 'em by the pussy' President in the Oval Office and those who follow him with sycophant obsession. But we also have the sword of Damocles feminine opportunists seeking to find offense where none exist and their emasculated masses of the sexually neutered. We live with social discourse that more resembles the gladiatorial refinement of thumbs up and down in the Coliseum in Rome than considered empathy and genuine understanding. We seek to hide behind affinities defined by tyrants rather than stand for considered, albeit lonely, principles. Gender, race, creed, affiliation, and association are more polarizing than they are merely the nuance of flourishing diversity. We're living in the shoot first, justify the shooting-without-asking-questions-later dystopia. This is not time for pandering. This is a time for locust-eating, sackcloth wearing prophet lizards to speak.

Which leads me to the words you'll find hemorrhaging from each page. As a young boy, 'truth' was a paradox. I was told that "the Word became Flesh," was the arbiter of 'truth' even though the Greek from which that 'truth' was translated bore no resemblance to the Hebrew or Aramaic from which it arose. I was encouraged to question but punished for the observations that failed to conform. And through all of this, I came to learn that the most insidious trap set by society to ensnare and enslave uses language as its primary weapon.

We cannot think without bumping up against the lexicon handed to us by manipulators and oppressors. And while some of you might have the impulse to congratulate yourself on your elevated consciousness— your post-Integral Turquoise—hold your golf clap.

The mere notion that we place on a linear or spiral scale our egoic projection of improving, social evolution across the illusory concept of time indicts our enslavement to artificial distinction of our own ascent without quantum consideration that *maybe 'we' are a retrograde version of human potential.* Put another way, we've adopted a narrative that places us at the zenith of 'development' or 'evolution' as though it's a one-way street and we're the 'best'. Is today 'better' than 'yesterday'? Is our culture, 'more advanced' than 100 years ago? How many times do we marvel at 'ancient wonders' and impose our tools of modernity on stones asking the question, "How did they (read, backward, less evolved, less technical) do it?" never considering that Egyptians or Inca may have had more advanced technologies lost to sands and jungles?

Karl Popper's amazing 1957 treatise on *The Poverty of Historicism* is one of the few times that we were given the opportunity to pause and consider that we may be trapping ourselves in our own illusion of our own story of ascent when we selectively ignore any evidence that doesn't substantiate our preeminence hypothesis. Is your Tesla more advanced than the Assyrian flying chariot? Is your antibiotic better than a healthy diet capable of sustaining life for over eight centuries?

A few pages ago, I unambiguously shared my contempt for pseudo-science. By this, I was specifically referring to the selective misapplication of science to reinforce a worldview that is thought too weak to stand on its own without the facade of scientific jargon. There will be those who will fairly criticize my following hypocritical exception. The scientific method and Science as a discipline is a dominant meme in today's society. Throughout this book, I will reference and critique what is generally accepted to be the world as understood by Science. Please understand that *all society believes to know is rationalized through a contrived narrative.*

Whether its gods, Periodic Tables of Elements or fallacies of quantum mechanics, *all naming conventions that seek distinction based on time or geometry are predicated on social illusions.* As neither time nor distance represent anything more than rational projections by people on an unassuming Universe, we know that all that is derived from those projections are simply consensus illusions. *E* does not equal *mc²* because light has no speed because speed requires distance and light is a coherent and perpetual energy. Ask a chemist or physicist from whence a neutron—a building block of all matter—comes and you'll rapidly see the mists of incredulity reminiscent of Papal pronouncements during the Inquisition.

I use scientific metaphors with their social resonant frequency alone—not implying any 'truth' derived therefrom. In other words, I'm using these terms so you can have a point of reference from which you can infer some meaning. I heartily commend my references to your consumption as some of them are perfectly fascinating.

And take a chill pill. The paragraph above just made some of your heads spin. Not because anything I said was that heretical but because it doesn't conform with the approved way we are told to see the world. Of course, there are shapes and geometry. Of course, there is distance. But is there?

For the past few thousand years, we have built a world defined by separation. In our creation myth, the first thing that happens is that 'light' and 'darkness' are put in opposition. Later comes water, air and land. Before long, we've got plants, animals and, last of all, humans. Ironically, the latest arrival on the scene gets the job of naming things—placing distinction on that which never agreed to be distinguished. Did the "giraffe" know that it was somehow distinct from the savanna? Did the cheetah know that it was a "predator", or did it see itself as the agent through which gazelles get to experience their feline power? In other words, are the edges really edges or did we put them there to control the story?

The trouble with this is that when the first words in the first story start with separation as a god-ordained mandate, how could any of us perceive a universe inextricably linked to itself? Worse still, how could we find our life's meaning when we say life starts at egg fertilization or at birth—two events which, while vitally important in the process of living, do not beget life. Remember that you are a perpetually living cell that just happened to replicate from an already living mother's egg and father's sperm.

Life IS.

Your experience as an organism is the continuation of two living cells that happened to meet through the act of reproduction. Put another way—*you aren't you*. You are a form of you-ness organized around a living energy seed that persisted in a timeless, dimensionless sense. And as we'll discuss in Chapter 1, our willingness to contemplate our phase in a timeless reality allows us to access information, power and purpose that individuated we could never reach.

I've organized this book in a chronology derived from our consensus myths of time. This presents a bit of a challenge as a fundamental thesis I advance is that time (like distance) is a perspectival lens but is not a reality. To the 21st century mind, this is the stuff of science fiction or quantum mumbo jumbo. In antiquarian Greek languages from Athens to Alexandria, this was a bit easier as there were verbs that were indefinite to time representing an always unfolding action. Many of the 'great' poets and philosophers we reference today had more words at their disposal than we do today placing an intriguing challenge of what is knowable. With fewer dimensions available in our language, communicating requires innovative approaches.

As such, in this book I will attempt triangulation. By this I mean that I will introduce an idea. Once unveiled, I'll attempt to expand on its intended meaning. Finally, I'll endeavor to use the idea in a story. Through these three perspectives, the intended outcome will be a more fulsome understanding of what I'm trying to convey. While this may feel cumbersome at times, just pat yourself on the back when you're frustrated and recognized that it's a sign you're just a quick learner!

So what motivates writing? Well, I've had many of these conversations with friends across the globe for most of my life. I am amazed at the overwhelming majority of people who, when confronted with wildly alternative perspectives whimsically muse about how nice it would be to "be able to think differently." When my film *Future Dreaming* debuted in Sydney in 2015, I frequently encountered those who said that they wished they could see the world I described in the film. While the film served as a lovely appetizer to whet the appetite, it did not afford the deeper conversation. So, this book is the main course.

In short, my desire is to seduce, cajole and incite you to think, react, and reflect, preferably with no particular end in mind. I would be disappointed if you found "belief" or "faith" in the end as I hold both in contempt. What I would find delightful is if, through these pages, you found a moment to sigh, ask a question or two that you have not dared to ask, and emerge from that question just a bit more light-hearted to embrace another glorious, ignominious, monotonous, dynamic day.

Let us, dear lizards, scamper on.

I

You Are a Star

꧁꧂

You didn't see that one coming, did you? A star? Really? Me? OMG!

But yes, there I said it. Book me on *Ellen* or *Oprah*.

I could have as easily said, "You are dust." But if I said that, you wouldn't have felt so sparkly or glowy now, would you? But telling you that you are a star is a great balance to the craziness of the preamble you just read. And let's face it, in the preceding section, I've undermined your excuse to be fat, thin, lazy, a nerd, a jock, an entrepreneur, an enlightened spirit fairy, a pretty unicorn mermaid, or whatever your thing is, so I should trump it with a star, baby!

Seriously, if you think of yourself as the meat, sinew and skin stretched across your bony carcass teeming with blood and other gooey substances ambling through each day—you're a star. That's for a bunch of reasons. First, the actual stuff you're made of—the molecules and atoms that organize you into the glorious being you are—are formed by atoms (what the Greeks called the indivisible or uncuttable). These atoms contain electrons that are the outer spinning bits, and the nucleus, comprised of protons and neutrons. And it's these last little guys that are an interesting puzzle. According to what's called the "Standard Model" (yes, you can go to Wikipedia and check this out), neutrons are produced when cosmic rays—pretty cool—interact with other stuff. Like the egg to the sperm, think of a giant cosmic penis having sex with the atmosphere or the dirt and—poof—baby neutrons. Which is pretty important because also according to science, neutrons hang around for between 10 and 14 minutes.

Now here's where it gets a bit dicey. Take a look at your fingernail. Unless you've got fake nails, you're looking at the chemical keratin which is made up of 28 carbon atoms, 48 hydrogen atoms, 2 nitrogen atoms, 32 oxygen atoms, and 4 sulfur atoms. Now buckle up. Just counting the neutrons in each of the atoms and counting all of their connections, you're going to have your mind blown with how many energetic connections are required to make a fingernail. If science is right that means that you have over 550 trillion energy connections to the union of stellar energy and other stuff in just the tip of your finger! And every 14 minutes, they reconnect.

If you're like me (and god help us if you are), you don't have room in your brain to think about those kinds of numbers. After all, it's busy connecting to quadrillions of other cosmic ray inspired energies right now and it simply ain't got time for the fingernail nonsense. But setting the numbers aside for a moment, just contemplate that no matter what version of science you embrace, that which turns into the flesh and blood we all are is a persistent energy that is born of stars. If any of the things we think we know are remotely correct, that fact is awe-inspiring!

From.

Think about this simple word. So simple. So innocent. Ah, not so fast. Where are you *from*? Where did we come *from*? Where did life *begin*? All of these exceptionally innocuous musings hold within them a world-view of separation. The notion that there is an origin is so deeply wired into our language (and its ontology) that we exclude the contemplation of a world without linear time or distance. We carelessly banter about the term 'creation' or 'creative' with ease without hearing within this an insidious inoculation to the possibility that everything and everyone always and perpetually exists.

When Lavoisier published the *Law of the Conservation of Mass* in 1789[1]—"In nature, nothing is created, nothing is lost, everything chang-

---

1. Antoine Lavoisier. *Traité élémentaire de chimie, présenté dans un ordre nouveau et d'après les découvertes modernes.* Paris, 1789.

es,"—he was thumbing his nose at thousands of years of religion that held that there was a creation—a beginning. Credited as the father of modern chemistry, his propositions were born of observations he made while measuring the effect of chemical reactions. And in his mathematics, his use of the notion of time was not some sort of linear clock. Rather he was considering 'time' as the movement of phases—an ever-unfolding reality in which matter simply passed through distinct expressions.

Place a piece of ice on your kitchen counter. Watch it. In all likelihood, you'll observe the chunk of ice slowly form a puddle. If you look closely, you'll see a bit of steam float up as the puddle grows. The water that was the piece of ice is not "changing". It's experiencing a plurality of phases (solid, liquid, vapor) but none of these fundamentally alter the chemistry of H_2O. All that happens is that the exact same molecules get to experience a variety of structures and properties. Lavoisier's observation was that the total quantity of 'water' doesn't *change* though its expression appears to alter.

Chaos (the precise phonetic expression of the Greek concept of 'emptiness' or 'void') *preceded* creation according to legend. In *Metamorphoses*, the Roman poet Ovid writes:

> *Before the ocean and the earth appeared— before the skies had overspread them all—*
>
> *the face of Nature in a vast expanse was naught but Chaos uniformly waste.*
>
> *It was a rude and undeveloped mass, that nothing made except a ponderous weight;*
>
> *and all discordant elements confused, were there congested in a shapeless heap.*

Sound familiar?

Trying to make sense of "beginnings", philosophers send their imagination into a common point or origins. Regardless of your religion or scientific affinity (equally a belief, mind you), we puzzle about a void *at the beginning*. But the irony is that we have to manufacture this narrative illusion because we can only imagine stories that 'start'. Is there really any difference between the Hebrew oral tradition codified in Genesis in the *Talmud*, Ovid, Homer, Hermes, or the 'Big Bang'? How did Ovid describe a "ponderous weight" which would infer a common narrative to the density of collapsing black holes when he didn't have Einstein to point the way? Our modern narrative of the Big Bang assumes *homogeneity* and *isotropy*. The former refers to the uniformity of stuff while the latter refers to the uniformity of dimension or orientation.

So even *before* everything, there's everything organized in perfect orientation? More simply, our most sophisticated models of a 'beginning' have an ordered pre-beginning. Sounds crazy, right? Absolutely. And the reason it sounds crazy is because it is an illusion rationalized with Greek mathematical symbols to dizzy the average reader into not asking the questions that would otherwise be asked.

So, ASK THE QUESTION!!!

Who is being served with a 'beginning' story?

If the inaccessible and erudite disciplines of physics and chemistry—really two sides of the same coin—are so necessary to confound the average observer, what on earth can be the energy that necessitates all this mythology? What is so damn important about *from*?

The answer may be really uncomfortable. Creation myths are told by those who wish to wield power and control. When you woke up this morning, no part of the sunrise required your assent or obedience. When you had your bowl of *Lucky Charms*—yes, my health food cereal of Saturday morning nutrition—your mitochondria didn't need to be motivated to metabolize those oh so yummy marshmallow unicorns. When you shuffled to the sink to brush your teeth in your fuzzy slippers, I'm certain you didn't contemplate the physics of how the toothpaste got into the tube. Here's a question: does *from* matter?

To you, probably not. So, to whom does it matter?

Well, let's think about who tells the stories.

One cannot avoid the most common purveyors of 'creation'—religion. Religion is predicated on *faith, hope, and belief.* These energies allow an ordinary person to place in someone else's control some, or all, of a life force. And before we ask the questions about motivations, let's examine these three concepts.

FAITH. Defined as "trust or confidence in someone or something," faith requires the assumption that your own existence, perception and experience is inadequate and must rely on an 'other'. For faith to flourish, inadequacy and lack of confidence must be manufactured through the art of intimidation or seduction. Who are the someones and what are the somethings that are supposed to be that in which we place our confidence?

That's where it gets really crazy. You're told to place faith in people who first must tell a story that you don't completely understand and then ask you to accept its importance. "They"—the gods, the aliens, the all-powerful Other, parents, politicians, teachers, clergy, the Pickles, associates—know something; They tell you part of their story (usually the part that requires you to feel inadequate at some level); and, then They ask you to place trust and confidence in their ability to look after you. You're not enough and you *need.* What do you need?

Well, that's unclear when faith is introduced. After all, these stories begin with inaccessible stories, myths and legends all placed in a 'before' which makes it perfectly clear that you—usually when you're young—could have no chance in verifying any piece of them. Once delivered—in recited story, song, or language—questioning is overtly or covertly prohibited. And by the time you're old enough to really think for yourself, your entire lexicon is delivered to you by those who seek your faith. Clever, isn't it? Someone creates the illusion into which you need to fit; forces you to accept that perspective as the 'right' one, and then asks you to place your faith in them or their worldview. The net effect—you surrogate your identity to another.

HOPE. This one's even more insidious. "An expectation or desire of an outcome," hope relies on a more dubious set of constructs. First of all, the present condition as it is, is insufficient. Through cunning manipulation, an illusion of a 'future' that has direction that is somehow 'good' can be held as a judge of the adequacy of the present. Like the Lorenz "Butterfly Effect", hope is nothing but a fallacy. Everything and every energy is present now. And now. And now…you get the point.

'Future' is a projection of an illusion of time but neither does nor can exist.

While phases can move in a transition, the notion that some act of will or intention can somehow alter the complex field effects of the ever-unfolding present is the fallacy of the flapping of the butterfly's wings. That something that is done now might have an impact on what happens next is possible. But far more likely, there is no effect—real or perceived. For the sake of clarity, if I burn a piece of wood from a pine tree, we can confidently state that said piece of wood cannot be used for building a table in the moment. But this observation only holds *in the moment*. The carbon dioxide from the burning of the soft pine may feed a growing oak tree (far better for furniture) with the passage of seasons. *To have hope is to judge the present as inadequate while holding the audacity that an unrealized 'future' will somehow improve upon the present.* Put another way, some condition of now would be better replaced.

Think about how many monotonous 'nexts' you have experienced in your life. For example, just when you finished reading the last sentence, an asteroid didn't wipe out all life on the planet… but in another galaxy, that just happened! Holy shit!

Would you be able to recognize 'better' when you're in the mindset that life in its present form is somehow not good enough? If you were to graph the most consequential moments in your life and attempt to draw a straight line through a rearward projection of 'past', you would need to selectively avoid *most* events to select those that forecast the consequential moments. That for which you "hoped", if it manifest, only did with your selective observation of that in the midst of many other things that you didn't contemplate—some which were better, some which were worse and *most that you didn't recollect at all*. And you would have no possible way to confirm (outside of your highly selective and curated memory) that any aspiration, intention, or effort had any impact on any 'next'.

Most importantly, if you habituate the notion that the present will be transcended by a 'better' 'other', the likelihood is extremely high that when you arrive at 'next', you'll find something 'wrong' with it as well.

BELIEF. What is 'belief'? In the end, it's an acceptance of the un-verifiable. Like faith, belief rests in a paradox. The notion is that someone else can create a construct to which you are meant to subscribe. Within that construct, you are to accept that there are 'knowns'—usually stuff that can be taken from you (time, loyalty, tithes, money, resources and other energies)—and 'unknowns'—usually ephemeral psychic 'benefits' that were made up by those who originated the construct in the first place. And the whole racket—designed for someone else's immediate benefit (fidelity, membership, control, influence, fame, power, etc)—is foisted upon you with the cunning use of 'belief'.

Three thousand years of modern philosophy and the religions that it has informed have been animated around the struggle between Kant's elucidation of the Greek notion of the noumenon—the essence of things—and phenomena—that which is apparent.[2] This distinction is a conceptual illusion of separation imposed by us on reality.

The notion that there's a 'why' or a 'mystery' beyond the observable is critical for the creation of gods, prophets, ancient astronaut theorists, and mystics. *The control of mystery is the agency of unspeakable power.* Convince someone that they're deficient for any reason—fallen angels, lowly estate, physically or mentally compromised, sinful, you name the label—and suddenly you control both the diagnosis and the cure. After all, against an anonymous comparison from an unexamined "ideal", deficiency is capricious. If you're not already unstable, we can find the

---

2. Immanuel Kant. *Prolegomena zu einer jeden künftigen Metaphysik, die als Wissenschaft wird auftreten können* Konigsberg. 1783.

dimension in which you're an abject failure. And the very diagnostician that pronounces you deficient has the remedy—a dependent belief. All it takes is your unquestioned assent to their world (and your duty to prop it up). The last part is the worst. If almighty gods and prophets were so relevant and omnipotent, doesn't it seem pathetic that they need adherents? If, as I was told as a child, "The Earth is the Lord's," one cannot help but conclude that he or she is a terrible steward of the mess that it's in. When you have to 'create' an illusion and then get yourself and others to animate it with agreement (and other, more material and profane things), you're a manipulative and controlling force. Believe me! NO, PLEASE DON'T. That's a joke.

Anonymous, remote, and unverifiable. These are the prerequisites to Faith, Hope, and Belief. *Without the illusion of separation in time and geography we could see things as they are.* We'd see that the writers of sacred texts were as concerned with salacious affairs, political influence, and oppression as they were with the propagation of wisdom. We'd see astrologers who calculated orbits and precessions before 'foretelling' omens to the uncalculating masses. We'd see murders rather than sacrifices. We'd see torture and cruelty. And we'd be a hell of a lot less likely to buy the bullshit. But make it 'a long time ago' in 'a land far far away' and suddenly every gilded relic enriches the storyteller.

It gets more comical in what we call science. In 2016, Attila Krasznahorkay announced that his team of researchers had isolated evidence of a fifth force of energy called X17. This energy that, as its name suggests had energy of 17 megaelectron volts, was seen to show up in light that was observed during lightning-induced isotopic decay of beryllium and helium—something that the Standard Model didn't account for[3]. For three years, 'peer review' has attempted to confirm these findings so that they can be published 'officially' despite their proliferation in media of lesser status. If they're 'right' according to the keepers of belief, belief will require alteration. So, who's to tell whether they correctly observed some-

---

3. https://www.popularmechanics.com/science/a29861192/fifth-force-nature/

thing or whether the inertia required to uphold belief will overwhelm that which challenges it?

To date, our model of the Universe is thought to explain what physicists estimate to be between 10-20% of the observable universe given our consensus means of observation. That means that between 80-90% of it is unexplained. And if the vast majority of what we know doesn't stand up to explaining what we observe in the 'in between', isn't it plausible that we don't know anything with certainty? Think about it: Our model of the Universe and its functioning can explain less than 20% of what we know must exist. Seventy-five percent to 90% of our DNA is "junk" according to Dan Graur from the University of Houston! That's right, what we 'know' about life is about 10-20% of the actual story!

Yet we don't consider the possibility that we are *blinded by the way we observe*. History is laden with irrefutable observations being official heresy because they undermine 'belief'. Heroes turn into villains. Saints become sinners. And how? Did any of their actions, thoughts or associations change? Of course not. What altered was the perspective through which they were observed. Belief—the currency of adherence-based loyalty—changed. And as a result, statutes are torn down; roads are re-named; and whole civilizations cease to hold relevance. All of science in our current era relies on time and distance. Both of these are agents of separation and distinction. And what our current models don't explain is how galaxies and stars hold *together*! Might we be perceiving everything through separation when the whole point is being together—all time, all space, all everything, all at once?

To be clear, this is not a tirade against good stories or fables. Wisdom can be as beneficial in parables as in the lived experience. The trouble is that when you're trying to understand your own reality, escaping the effects of a society so deeply built on Faith, Hope and Belief is a massive undertaking. Ironically, a genuine perspective on what is real may benefit from a literal 'fast' from words.

See if you can observe the world without naming what you see. See if you can blur your eyes just a bit and "see" this page without "seeing" words. Can you suspend that part of your cognition that must 'make sense' long enough to see shapes? ✎☜■ ◰□◆ ◆◆◆□♏■♌♌ ◆ ♒☜◆ □☜□◆ □✗ ◰□◆□ ♏□♓♌■✂◆✂□■ ◆♒☜ ◆ ○◆◆◆ ❻○☜&♏ ◆♏■◆♏❼ ●□■♌ ♏■□◆♌ ♒ ◆□ ◆♏♏ ◆♏☜□♏◆? You're welcome. I just showed you the immediately preceding sentence in the wingdings font! Its meaning is the same. You just weren't trained in deciphering computer glyphs.

In all of life, actively engaging observation that is not the sanctioned one (see a taste, feel a sound, smell a touch) stretches the power of observation and allows for the consideration that we might use 'belief' merely as a lazy excuse to stop working on understanding. It's hard not to reduce input stimuli into apparent 'meaning'. That said, it's the only way to hold life in equanimity (the absence of judgment) and figure out what is really going on.

By now we've felt the vertigo of realizing that "THEY" (our all-knowing smart people) may not 'know' much. They are spending hundreds of millions of dollars on magnets, refrigeration, optical and electromagnetic sensors, computers, and bright doctoral students to unravel a mystery of *their own creation*. And we marvel when they tell us that they've collided stuff into stuff and the dust from the collision includes quarks and bosons (like any of us care)! They also tell us that they didn't see what should have shown up and some of what they detected wasn't in the plan. We go back to whatever we were doing and we wait for a few more years before we find out that THEY still don't quite have it together.

Try this on for size. What if the fundamental error was *from*? What if we didn't have a start or an end? What if light just is—not millions of light years away? What if that which holds you together is the same thing that holds galaxies together? What if the glue that is you is actually what is holding together that which you observe? If we all stopped looking, would any of the observed still hang around?

Sit with this for a moment. If you are the continuation of the messy orgasm that your mom and dad had in the back of a station wagon, on a beach, or in a fluffy bed, with one half of your chromosomal cosmic antenna picking up signals that your dad was tuning into and the other half those of your mom, did you really 'begin' or are you the product of two perspectives converging? If you look at the chromosomes that are in sperm and eggs when they go through fertilization, you see that in the first moment they first replicate, the little fingers of chromosomes line up as though reacting to a magnet. When the first cell replicates into two identical cells, that 'magnetic' effect happens again. And again. And again. Before long, shape starts emerging but all from the subtle magnetism of cell replication.

Friedrich Miescher stumbled across white blood cell proteins that had unusually high phosphorus content when examining pus-filled bandages in 1869. What he was looking at was chemistry that was part of what we now think of as DNA. Long before James Watson and Francis Crick described the three-dimensional double helix we think of as DNA in 1953, many researchers were figuring out that some part of the cell's chemistry was responsible for signaling what the cell was to be and what it was to do. Remember, function—a phase condition—didn't mean a differentiated organism. Whether it's phosphorus pus, DNA or imaginal discs, nature is filled with templates for the phase that's coming. It just meant that some complete code of intent was organizing so it could organize. Like the quarks in the cosmos, the way DNA was described was by taking it *out of its natural context* and trying to observe system dynamics in controllable segments. What we 'know' about life is based on a worldview that celebrates the explanation of a little bit and then belief about the whole.

The trouble with this idea is that DNA doesn't naturally come in a long thread. Instead it comes in a tightly coiled bundle called a chromosome. And if you know anything about taking a charged conductor and winding it into a coil, you realize that by doing so, you form an antenna. That's right, that wound up coiled mass that signaled your arrival can receive and transmit a radio signal. You picked up signals from the universe *and transmitted to the universe that you were here!*

Now, before you become your own DJ, settle down. Yes, you are picking up your favorite indie band in your left toe right now. And no, you can't necessarily hear it on your Bluetooth speakers. But that doesn't change the fact that the organism that you are is sensitive to electromagnetic spectrum.

If we were to reflect on other cultures, many scholars marvel at 'primitive' obsessions with the stars. Mayans had their observatories and calendars. Incas had their mirrored models of the celestial landscape. Egyptians aligned monuments to precessing constellations. Chinese and Indus communities planted and harvested under favorable moons. Birds transect the hemispheres while calving whales swim below them. Sunflowers face their namesake as it slips across the sultry summer sky. Regardless of the phase of social interaction, that which happens above is seen to influence that which unfolds below and vice versa.

Imagine how we'd live if we saw ourselves as an inextricable union with conjoining planets, swirling galaxies, and blooming flowers. What if the sun didn't know it was 93 million miles 'away' and thought that it was as important to us as we were to it? What if auspicious times to plant, have sex for procreation, harvest, move, and remain were perceived by humans tuned into the whole of universal energies, not those that pretend to "understand" 20% and remain clueless about 80% of the energies that influence everything? What if the stones that were hewn and stacked in Peru were shaped with today's elusive "Dark Matter"? What if our callous indifference towards our natural world actually deafens that which that world seeks to share with us for our own good?

I started this chapter with a cute statement: You are a star! But now I'm getting dead serious. If we didn't define a world based on difference, based on 'from', based on the remote, the unverifiable, and the anonymous, we may realize that we are an INDIVISIBLE contributor to the whole of the universe and without our participation, the possibility for the whole is lessened.

What if you don't matter to your job, your family, your spouse? Rather you are inseparably necessary to their very existence and they to yours. And what if we saw ourselves as energy sensors and transmitters—always activating and always receiving—rather than seeing ourselves as the cul-de-sac of self-fulfillment? Might your worthless feelings come from the perception that as a separate, individuated actor, you've forced yourself into detached irrelevance? By obsessing about the 'froms' in our story, we've handed our relevance over to others who have neither thought nor consideration for our lives. Might your path to meaning commence with a recognition that you are not alone? You've got a whole Universe counting on you!

II

You Are What You Eat

꧁ꕥ꧂

I don't know if it happened in your family, but at some point before I learned that we were really having liver because 'it was that time of the month' for my mom (you know, need more iron and all), I'd be told, "You are what you eat." The thought of being a yucky liver was disgusting. The thought of needing a dietary accommodation for your mom's period…not much better! I hated liver then. Knowing that it's part of a sympathetic menstrual diet did nothing to change my aversion to liver to this day.

My go-to food earned me the name "Gravy Davy" for years. Any guesses what I loved to eat? Mashed potatoes and gravy! But if you would ask me what I loved the most when I was five, my answer would have been chocolate and at 52…*still chocolate!* And before we fall into the predictable truisms that plague every dinner table that ever tried to pass broccoli off as a yummy alternative to, well, let's just say, chocolate, there are a million ways I could take the "are what you eat".

For the record, gout physician Anthelm Brillat-Savarin is credited with the coining of the phrase in 1826[1]. That's right, a dude studying gout had a hunch that his patients' diets *may provide a little hint to their ailment —gout!* Genius, right? He also stated that, "Dessert without cheese is like a pretty girl with one eye," and, "What women will, God wills..this in five words is the whole Parisian charter." I have no idea what the hell those phrases meant to 19th century France but they would cer-

---

1. Anthelm Brillat-Savarin. *Physiologie du Gout, ou Meditations de Gastronomie Transcendante.* Paris. 1826

tainly score on the creepy factor in 2020!

It's likely that you don't know New York public relations personality Oberon Sinclair. What's far less likely would be your immunity to her effect. That upon which butterflies feast (yes, we're going to keep this going the whole book) is that which Oberon wanted you to eat too. Kale! Like the creation of orange juice after the bumper crop of 1907 by Lord & Thomas, Ms. Sinclair decided that you and I should eat kale. Celebrities dressed in it, actresses breathlessly hawked it on morning television shows, and science extolled that which the simple white cabbage butterfly —*Pieris rapae* —has always known. Kale is good for caterpillars wanting to become butterflies! And organic kale —*no, say it ain't so, Dave, could such bliss exist?* —is the bee's knees, baby! Cold pressed, juiced, chopped into salads for part of a green, vital, vegan life, can there be anything that isn't beatified by that green goodness? Obviously not.

Except for the tiny little tadpole of concern that the mass production of organic kale (and industrial heathen, godless kale from unconscious growers) often benefits from the application of *Bacillus thuringiensis* (or *Bt*) for pest (read butterfly) control. And I know that this couldn't have any association at all, but the bacterium *Bt* creates a crystalline toxin that attacks the gut in insects leading to leaky guts and bowel disruption. Since the Japanese isolated *Bt* in 1901 and since its wholesale adoption in industrial agriculture by the 1930s and 40s, this could have nothing to do with the rapid rise in irritable bowel syndrome, food allergies, or epidemic food sensitives because scientists at the Environmental Protection Agency told us that it is 'safe', right?

Whatever you do, don't read the little article from Italy referenced below, which attracted no attention, that refuted the assertion that *Bt* only disrupts the intestines of insects[2]. And whatever you do, don't read it while eating an organic kale salad, drinking pomegranate juice and washing it all down with juiced celery. You might conclude that you are certainly defined by what you eat and how often you run to the toilet!

---

2. Finamore A, et al. *"Intestinal and peripheral immune response to MON810 maize ingestion in weaning and old mice." J Agric Food Chem.* Dec 10;56(23):11533-9.

During my training in physiology, one of my favorite parts of the cell was the mitochondria. I think it was because all the diagrams of mitochondria looked like the old school lava lamps that were popular during my adolescence. To think that these little blobby things could basically hold within their cool cartoon-looking structures the balance of life and death still fascinates the hell out of me. Referred to as organelles (you've got this one —they're like little organs in the body), mitochondria are considered the primary location where respiration and energy production take place in the body. And, spoiler alert, they are living proof that your mom, your dad, and Anthelm were wrong —at least for the most part. While mitochondria have their very own form of DNA (how cool is that?), they basically have the job of unlocking sunlight in your body.

Hold on! Unlocking sunlight? What does that mean?

Once again, in our elaborate scientific belief system, sun shines on leaves, leaves convert photons into chemical energy linking one carbon atom to a 5-carbon ring and, presto chango!, we get glucose. This 6-carbon molecule is what we eat. And for all you carbon haters —here's some bad news. EVERYTHING that energizes and animates you is, you guessed it… CARBON!

Side note, when I do eat *Lucky Charms*, I'm just treating my mitochondria to some easily accessible glucose, so take that you health nuts! Regardless of what you shove into the pie hole in your face, your mitochondria are going to 'eat' the same thing —sugar! What a sweet life! And you can make that job hard or easy —still no different to the mitochondria. Honey they want…honey they get!

Now before you sit down on the couch and eat a container of Oreos or chocolate pudding, don't think that how you get those glucose molecules is somehow irrelevant. There are a host of intermediaries —both tissue and chemical —in your digestion process that can be profoundly and adversely impacted by diets that are not appropriately selected. That said, whether your yoga instructor believes it or not, you're a sugar powered machine… how sweet it is!

Let's go back to the photosynthesis sunlight thingamajiggy. This whole "you are what you eat" thing needs a closer examination. Carbon dioxide and water —rather prolific molecules —are part of an important perpetual motion machine that keeps us in the business of eating and breathing. I think that we're good with both of these ideas, aren't we? Well, to hear scientists tell the magical story, when light hits chloroplasts (also organelles, this time in plants), water is split apart releasing oxygen (the one you just breathed just then) and harvesting the energy from hydrogen dissociating. This energy is used to synthesize glucose by putting atmospheric carbon dioxide (the stuff you just breathed out) into existing carbon molecules that are just hanging out in leaves. This process —known as the Calvin cycle (surprisingly named for the dude that won the Nobel Prize in 1961 before which no life existed as we know it) —uses many of the exact same biochemical intermediaries that are part of the mitochondria's unlocking process. The unlocking process in the mitochondria —known as the Krebs cycle (surprisingly named for the dude that won the Nobel Prize in 1953 before which no human could eat sugar) —produces the very carbon dioxide that the plants need to do the synthesis all over again. So funny enough, plants don't get their CO_2 without us breathing out our mitochondrial by-product and we don't get oxygen and glucose without plants putting out. So, who is eating whom?

Which came first, the chicken or the egg?

I don't know but after all this, it just seemed like a good question to pose! Oh and while I'm at it, here's a little non sequitur: why does everybody who is trying to get you to eat vegan still say that things that taste good taste like bacon? Weird, don't you think?

What I like about the mitochondria and chloroplast story is the interdependence that this story tells. When we think about the question of separation, boundaries or distinction, seeing the dynamic that begets what we've decided is life on this planet defies our myth of separation. Flora and fauna are not separate. In fact, they are explicitly and inseparably bound. Maybe we should say we are what eats us!

Living in 21st century society, identity around food is one of the most clearly demarcated classifications. What you eat defines who you are. Nothing could place this in more dramatic relief than the urban vegetarian or vegan. Suggesting that spinal cords and brains somehow serve as the arbitrary line of 'living' or 'sentience' confirms the capricious dominion myth that has enslaved humanity for at least the last four thousand years of storytelling. Day-threers (as I like to call my veggie friends) seem to need to make it clear that Day-fivers (birds and fish) and Day-sixers (land dwellers) are somehow more cruel or inhumane. Making up fantastical tales about the shape of molar teeth and the evolutionary propensity to eat grains and greens somehow signifies a greater sense of spirituality than looking at the canine teeth evidenced in every smile and musing about their bloody, sharp tearing utility.

Now canines can crack open husks to keep the green theme going. What troubles me is NOT vegetables and fruits. My diet is primarily thus. What does trouble me is the notion that somehow plants are devoid of sentience or that somehow the biochemistry of the biome in our gut provides justification for dogma. Green is likely good! But blind assent to 'green' without a modicum of disclaimer on the profligate abuse of toxins in the supply chain is hardly conscious. And for the enterprising reader —have a look at what you can spray on food and still call it 'organic'. You wouldn't eat much of it!

But let's hop in our time machine (since time is an illusion anyhow, let's have another illusion of a time machine, shall we?) and spin into other eras or locations of the human story. Let's go back, um, about 7 years. I had the great fortune of spending time in the Gobi Desert with Bud. Bud, and his father, and his father's father, and his father's father's father (you get the point) herd camels. I was invited to be his guest for a week.

Now if you haven't been to the Gobi Desert in Mongolia, I'll do my best to paint a picture. Think mostly sand and brown dirt. There, you've got it. That was easy.

Now look out on the horizon and imagine a faint green hue. Cool.

While you're standing where you are, you see basically sand and brown dirt. But if you look far enough into the distance —pretty easy, since the horizon in the Gobi Desert is the optical curvature of the earth or about 3.5 miles —the green hue is from the extremely sparse grass that lives in the inhospitable terrain. Camels eat that grass. And like other ruminant beasts, they eat the grass roots and all, meaning that they get some bites of dirt free inside (remember this because it's important later).

Now Bud, his family and his camels graze about 70 miles of desert each day. Every so often they move 140 miles, pitch their gur (a camel felt tent) and then graze, 70 miles in one direction, then another two days later, and so forth until they've grazed out the area. Then they move again. They've been doing this for centuries. And for reasons I asked but could never understand, their turnaround point on the eastern extreme is less than 20 miles from a massive oasis flowing with water and covered in lush grass. They never go there. Never have. Just back and forth across the barren desert.

Now guess what! Bud and his family eat nothing but that which the camel provides. Camel milk, yogurt, butter, cheese, arkhi (spoiled milk vodka) and, you guessed it, camel. While he's tending his camel and caring for his family, Bud has countless hours to reflect on the cosmology that he's learned from his forebearers —observations that center around the *Great Blue Sky*. Do you wonder what animates his reverent worship of the blue sky? Because he's part of it. He, his family, and his camels the way they've done it for timeless time. You know what none of Bud's family have? Food allergies. Obesity. Diabetes. Or many of the other life-style 'diseases' embraced by enlightened beings. Oh, and he doesn't eat kale.

Whether it's camel in the Gobi Desert, fresh water eel steamed in gourd vines and coconut in the Komgi in East New Britain, Papua New Guinea, pecan pie (with chocolate chips) in Virginia, or miso in Japan, our identification around food says a lot about our actual living. *When that which we consume is coherent with the place in which we find ourselves, something about the sustenance and something about the suit-*

ability of that sustenance to its environment go hand in hand. When navigators seeking the Northwest Passage died of scurvy and other diet-related illnesses, how was it that the Inuit in the same environment persisted? Harsh conditions? No. Failure to live in coherence with life where you find it? Yes.

Is it any wonder that our urban living places us in abject confusion? I can rock up to Whole Foods or Wegmans and expect to purchase pineapple, kiwi, Chilean seabass, cassava, Swiss cheese, Costa Rican coffee, free-range eggs of all sorts, and kale from anywhere on earth at any time of the day. And while we can find ourselves indifferent to the asymmetries that this represents, *do we take the time to consider that our food dissonance may impact the quality and quantity of life we enjoy?*

Somewhere in the 1940s and 50s when industrial agriculture replaced agro-awareness —thought to be born in the fertile alluvial fields between the Tigris and Euphrates Rivers over 10,000 years in rearward projection of the time illusion —we stepped out of phase with the growing cycles and seasons of our localities. Rather than having a hand in the planting, weeding, shepherding, harvesting, storing and preparing of things, we broke our connection with our sustenance. Urban vegans can voraciously consume beans and peas thinking they're devoid of sentience and soul because they haven't stepped barefoot into the cool morning dirt and felt the pendulous sweet pea ripe for harvest and marveled at its beauty. No soul? Not a chance.

You see that the challenge we confront is another by-product of the separation story. Whether it's slaughtering a cow, pig or fish, whether it's water-bath sealing a jar of peaches, whether it's knocking the butterfly caterpillar off a cabbage, when you detach from your sustenance, you can imagine dominion or hierarchy on other living things —both flora and fauna. When your hands are covered with blood, cream, dirt or dew, you can recognize the entanglement of living and reverence any and all of it. In the real places I've traveled in my time machine where humanity lives in coherence with its sustenance, I have not observed waste, over-production or obese artifacts of over-consumption. *You're not what you eat as much as you are defined by your connection to your sustenance.*

I told you to remember the camel's proclivity to eat grass all the way down to the roots. By doing this, the camel is actually eating some of the dirt. The dirt in the Gobi Desert is filled with considerable amounts of metals and salts. As a result, all that is 'camel' (milk, meat, sinew) includes enormous quantities of salt.

Side note: when I was a young man, we lived on a little farm in Southeastern Pennsylvania. Each Spring when we'd let the cows, sheep and goats out to graze for the first time after winter, the milk would take on the taste of garlic and onion for about a week as that's what the animals grazed first. This was great if you were making potato leek soup but positively dreadful if you wanted to make ice cream (with chocolate, of course).

Back to the camels eating dirt. Humans have exploited the camel's ability to persist in arid, salty climates for extended periods of time. While most animals would experience vascular failure, dehydration and death when they lose about 12% of their blood volume, camels have been shown to function with losses nearly three times that amount.[3] Ironically, based on access to food, water, and ambient conditions such as heat, the camel actually alters its chemistry to thrive in the environment in which it finds itself. While most of us would think of salt making us thirsty, the camel cleverly uses salt as a way to hold onto water. And by eating its environment, it becomes capable of persisting in that environment where other animals —like us —would perish. You are *where* you eat, maybe?

I'll never forget the first time I was heckled by a cannibal. I was asked to speak at an event coordinated by the Pacific Island Forum Secretariat —the mini-U.N. of the 14 island nations in the Pacific Ocean. Samoa hosted the gathering themed around the notion of *innovation*. In hindsight, I should have suggested that I be a keynote listener rather than speaker as I found the stories of local customary practice positively capti-

---

3. B. Schmidt-Nielsen, et al. *"Water Balance of the Camel." American Journal of Physiology.* 185(1):185-194. 1956.

vating. When I got up to speak, I launched into an epic revival-preacher style story of a world in which colonialism never set foot on the pristine Pacific Islands and that healers and communities were allowed to live undefiled by the Europeans that brought their gods, their gunpowder, their greed and diseases. At the crescendo of my speech, I said, "Imagine if I was the first outsider to step on your shores 300 years ago," when I was immediately interrupted by a man in the back of the hall.

"We would eat you," he shouted triggering uproarious laughter and applause.

Without missing a beat, I replied, "Since this is the first time I've been heckled by a cannibal, I'd like to settle a question that I've pondered for too long. Would I be best roasted or steamed?"

"You don't have enough fat on you to roast," he replied. "We'd wrap you up in banana leaves, put hot stones in your belly, and steam you for a day or two. Then the meat comes right off the bones."

After I finished my somewhat modified speech with a modicum of greater humility, I approached the man in the back of the room. We set into a long conversation about how several island communities, including his own, had, from time to time, found people to be the most convenient source of nutrition. I love to think of myself as open-minded, but I must confess that I struggled with the casual discussion of eating someone from your neighboring tribe like we'd talk about stopping off at a fast food restaurant. Worse still was the notion that, during certain times, a local kid was lunch because there were plenty running about and more could be made. But this conversation, while jarring, was so deeply fascinating that I found it captivating. I was eating up every word. Yes, I *did have to go there because the pun was wanting to be written*. What struck me in the conversation was the degree to which he implied that eating a person wasn't their end but rather their perpetuation as a part of the whole community. In short, by consuming someone, *they persisted*.

Which set my thoughts in motion. Do we "consume" food or are we merely part of the process whereby energy and matter transitions through phases? If the camel and the kangaroo can live in scorching desert heat by having their body chemistry alter to become a desert, are they "consuming" or are they participating with their symbiotic ecosystem? Is it not likely that the poo that they produce is actually the seed of the grass as much as the grass was the nutrition they took in? As the egg is to the larvae is to the pupae, so may be the process of digestive interactions on a macro level. Think of the lizard that eats the spider in the desert. Between crickets and spiders, many times the lizard's choice of the spider is because it contains more water than the cricket. But is it extinguishing the spider when it eats it or is it taking on the essence of the spider and is the spider engaging its lizard experience?

When the gazelle starts running in front of the advancing lion, is it predator and prey as we have been trained to see, or is the gazelle pumping hot warm blood into its muscles to marinate the feast that the lions will share? Some snakes have paralytic toxins so that they consume their diets while the diet is still very much alive. Others squeeze the breath out of their meals before consuming them. There can be no question that in both cases, variations in the chemistry of digestion is a function of the preparatory condition of that which is taken in.

In the Kantemo Bat Cave, isn't it fascinating that the snakes that catch bats do so by hanging from the ceiling…like bats? Did they 'learn' from the bats or is there a hanging essence of bats that the snakes literally incarnate? As long as we're talking about CO_2 and water, we don't mind seeing ourselves as part of the tree's life cycle. When we take it up in scale, we get creeped out. Somewhere after the fertilizer value of poo, we don't want to think of ourselves as being part of other life energy dynamics. After all, we're the dominion holders —not the lesser animals and plants, right?

Umm… Dave, you're making us very uncomfortable here…

All I'm doing is making an observation at scale and that alters perspective rather dramatically.

Settle down for a moment! I'm not saying that the predation / prey dynamic is in error. But I am asking the question whether we fully understand what we truly are in the big scheme of things? That we see ourselves as the exclusive beneficiary of what we eat is a worldview in which our sustenance is the point.

If we saw ourselves as an energetic transition enabler —taking food and moving it through phases into CO_2, water, and nutrients that other life forms will ingest, would we be more considerate of what and how we ate? And if we saw ourselves as integrating proteins, fats and carbohydrates (all coiled conductive chemical transmitters and receivers) from other life forms into ourselves, would we possibly be more discriminating on understanding the nature of what we eat? When my Andean friends speak of the llama, they don't refer to it as a commodity that they consume. Rather they reverence it as an inextricable part of their community and their spirit.

Nostalgia? Maybe. But maybe they understand things that our 'modern' indifference ignores. And maybe the *Bt* kale, the hydroponic tomato, and the force-fed filet are actually telling us an extinction story of unconsidered gluttony to which some attention should be paid.

You're not healthy because you eat vegan. You're not fat because you eat McDonalds burgers and fries. You are not *what* you eat. More appropriately, your life and your diet reflect the level of consciousness and care you apply to your living. Unconsidered consumption of kale or Krispy Kreme is an external manifestation of internal lack of sensitivity to your place within your ecosystem. And whether your saturated fats clog your arteries, or your vegetable obsession fuels immigrant labor repression in fields across the world, the sclerotic effect on your consciousness is the same.

III

You Are Where You Live

When I was a little boy in Upland California, I watched Dr. Louis Leakey's epic tale of his explorations of Tanzania's Olduvai Gorge. In National Geographic's *Dr Leakey and the Dawn of Man*, the opening sequence states:

> *"Out of the darkness rushed a strange creature spurred by hunger to drive the vultures away."*

In the grainy video, we see a flock of vultures feasting on an anonymous hunk of carrion and a lone man running towards said vultures to 'steal' their feast. In stark contrast to the evidence he found, including massive caches of tools and evidence of abattoirs complete with a variety of skeletal remains of the butchered at places like Oldowan, the film places this running hominid in an abstraction of prehistoric brutality. Estimated to be anywhere between hundreds of thousands and 1.4 million years old, the Leakey contribution to Darwin's work sought to pinpoint the 'beginning' of humans—the 'birthplace' in the heart of Africa.

As I addressed in the Prologue, the question of *from* is an obsession animated by a notion that evolution is a linear, cumulatively beneficial trajectory with each age somehow improving on what came 'before'. Not surprisingly, from the *Bible*'s Eden to Leakey's Olduvai, *from where* serves to place in a locality that which we expect to inform something about *who*. Think of it. Have you ever heard of naked islanders frolicking on the beach drinking from coconuts during the Ice Age? Were Zoroastrians zipping around in flying Mazda *zoom-zoom* crafts when the Ezekiel saw flying gyroscopes during the Israelite exile in Babylon a few hundred years before Greek and Roman charioteers conquered what is now Iraq and Iran? With each phase of dominant 'historical narrative' *where* you're from dictates the capabilities you must possess.

Not far from the Sinivit Gold Mine just south of Rabal, Papua New Guinea there is a large flat mountaintop. Curiously, the perimeter of this spot is marked with immense holes hewn deep into the rock. The local legend tells the following story.

Before the lands broke apart, everyone lived in harmony on the verdant island. On Naski—the original mountain—people decided that they wanted to build a very tall tower. Digging deep holes into the volcanic rock, they placed poles from the great trees of the forest and bound these poles to the great tree in the middle of the native garden. Supported by the great central tree and the sturdy foundation, people kept building the tower higher and higher into the heavens. The story gets a bit wobbly here, but for some reason, people started disagreeing (about what?, who knows?) and that conflict spread throughout the builders. As they grew frustrated, a great earthquake came and split the land forcing the sea to rush in and separate the land. This event happened so quickly that different families were left drifting apart and thus, earth's continents and cultures were divided. One day, according to the myth, the horn-billed toucan and the bird of paradise will fly across Naski and pull the lands back together and with it, reunite humanity.

Now read the *Genesis* account of the Tower of Babel.

> [1] *And the whole earth was of one language, and of one speech.*
>
> [2] *And it came to pass, as they journeyed from the east, that they found a plain in the land of Shinar; and they dwelt there.*
>
> [3] *And they said one to another, Go, let us make brick, and burn them thoroughly. And they had brick for stone, and slime had they for mortar.*

4 And they said, Go, let us build us a city and a tower, whose top may reach unto heaven; and let us make us a name, lest we be scattered abroad upon the face of the whole earth.

5 And the LORD came down to see the city and the tower, which the children of men were building.

6 And the LORD said, Behold, the people is one, and they have all one language; and this they begin to do: and now nothing will be restrained from them, which they have imagined to do.

7 Go, let us go down, and there confound their language, that they may not understand one another's speech.

8 So the LORD scattered them abroad from thence upon the face of all the earth: and they left off to build the city.

9 Therefore is the name of it called Babel; because the LORD did there confound the language of all the earth: and from thence did the LORD scatter them abroad upon the face of all the earth. — Genesis 11:1–9

While the post code of your birth has considerable effect on the myths you'll be told, the essence of your myths, your language and your values are remarkably predictable based on our current understanding. You probably have *qi* that is polarized as *yin* and *yang* in one of hundreds of variants. You probably have celestial jealousy that is angered by the precociousness of humans. You probably have movement from one land to another or the literal cleaving of lands. And you have Babel, Naski, Etemananki, Kongo Moon Poles, great Pagodas and all manner of super-structures somehow seeking to ascend to the heavens.

Or you maybe have anthropologists who see diagrams and stories from other cultures and ascribe common narratives to make the foreign sound familiar, albeit primitive. Oops, I shouldn't have added that last bit. Was similarity extant or did we impose it on our constructions of the narratives of others? More simply, are cultures similar in their myths and stories or do we interpret past symbols and stories through the lens of our own in an attempt to link to or improve upon our projection of antiquity? Do paintings in Egyptian tombs signify "final judgements" or celestial deities or did the archeologists who interpreted their meaning shape their interpretation through the lens of their social narratives?

Now that I've suggested that we may be the architects of the re-narrating of stories in a form that suits our perspective thereby indicting pretty much all we are told to believe (there's that nasty little word again), it may be prudent to take the pot off the stove and cool things down a bit, shall we?

Let's think of the animal kingdom for a moment. Phew. Thanks. This last bit was making me feel a bit woozy.

Nature, as we know it on TV, couldn't exist but for the very British voice over provided by Sir David Attenborough. Between Attenborough and Morgan Freeman, nary a penguin could waddle, a cheetah run, nor a ruby throated hummingbird suckle nectar from a flower but for their beguiling voice narrating the very action into existence. That Charles Darwin even made it to the Galapagos Islands without the aid of these two narrators boggles the mind.

In *On the Origin of Species*, Darwin paints a picture that implants in modern thought the certitude that, in the struggle for existence, immediate survival is dependent on the fittest in any environment not only surviving in its habitat but subtly evolving to adapt to the same. While seeking to abolish the Adamic origin story on the one hand, Darwin was equally obsessed with classification systems as was the Adam myth's fixation on naming everything. In both instances, the assumption that *place* influenced *essence* and *expression* is pervasive. Further, in both stories, one doesn't have to go very far to find that life is a constant battle between resources and those who can command them.

Which brings me to one of my favorite puzzles. Does the insect look like a stick, the striped tiger look like the reedy marsh, or the chromatophore laden chameleon look like the leaf in camouflage or does it perceive and adapt to an isomorphic condition? Whoa, you just dropped a big word bomb on us and didn't warn us! Damn it, Dave. If you want us to read this book, don't force us to buy a dictionary too.

O.K., cool down partner.

Isomorphism just means having equal or equivalent form. To put it in *Mr. Roger's Neighborhood* or *Sesame Street* terminology, "one of these things is *just like* the other." So when we see an insect that looks like a stick, Attenborough and Freeman lower their voice into a hushed, urgent tone insinuating that we shouldn't point out the poor unsuspecting animal that, if detected, will be eaten by that....LOOK OUT! THERE'S A SWOOPING BIRD ABOUT TO... Whew, close call! We figure that animals take on the image of their environment to hide—either as predator or prey.

What if the butterfly that looks like a leaf or flower has that look because the leaf or flower looks like it? What if, by looking like the thing, you don't get eggs laid on you, caterpillars eating you, and chrysalis hanging off you? Who said that the insect looked like the stick? Did the tiger's stripes make it blend in with the marshy grasses or did the grass grow in stripes to allow the ecosystem to remain in balance? *Like our discussion of food in the previous chapter, we've insisted that the perceived higher or more complex life form adapts to the lower life or inanimate form's visible expression without contemplating that the 'natural selection' flow may be reversed or may be entirely irrelevant.*

Whether it's the reptile eggs that select gender based on the ambient temperature, the animals that alter their biology to embrace their access to food and water or people who variously live above the ground, in caves (natural and hewn from the rock), in trees, or in houses and apartments, we've adopted a perspective that defines 'who' by where. If you live in a 50-story high-rise, you're somehow 'more advanced' than the person who rolls out a palm mat on the sand. And to be sure, your physical habitat defines some of the selections you make in other areas of living. Beijing, Tokyo, and New York hardly afford access to loamy soil in which you can grow vegetables. And while we've been told that dense in-fill housing is somehow a mark of modernity, when one replaces soil and vegetation for concrete, glass, and asphalt, this decision comes at a cost.

In 1993, Richard Auty coined the term "resource curse" upon observing the propensity for mineral and energy rich countries to have profligate corruption and abject poverty. This observation—while given a catchy name—has been made for as long as the Spanish, British, and Dutch Conquistadors and Trading Companies plundered the world for the isolated few artifacts of imperial value. When Adam Smith wrote his manifesto on *An Inquiry into the Nature and the Causes of the Wealth of Nations* in 1776 (wait, I thought America owned that year with its independence and all), he delineated the world of the 'civilized' in contrast to the barbarous, the savage and the heathen.

What made a place civilized and another savage? Simple, if selected metals, foods, or energy stores were remote to those that wished to possess them and the would-be possessors had the agency of appropriation—swords, gunpowder, disease, religion, etc.—those who 'took' were 'civilized' and those from whom the taking happened were barbarian. Smith was clear that the mark of civilization was the 'division of labor'. If a place in Africa, Asia, or the Americas didn't have an industrial hierarchy that was apparently identical to those of Europe, clearly, the place was heathen. While not expressly stated, he described a world in which an 'other' defined desires and needs, developed the infrastructure to barter their satiation with labor and wages, and preserved ample separation from both the 'industrialist' who held the terms of capital and power, and the remote heathen from whom 'raw materials' were taken.

By telling the consumer that they 'needed' sugar, coffee, silk, steel, tobacco, opium and numerous other vices and virtues, exploiting the mass ignorance gap between those who needed to fit the social ideal and those who enabled the supply thereof, social structures rallied justification for scourges like slavery, combat, genocide—behaviors as prevalent today as they were 400 years ago. Was the Spanish conquest of Mexico any different from the Belgian genocide in Rwanda[1] or Rio Tinto's civil war in Bougainville?[2]

I often find myself bristling at the faux empathy expressed by NGOs, 'development' organizations, and charities as they seek to 'advance' societies from which great wealth has been expropriated to placate artificial 'needs' of thoughtless consumers. "They don't even have [*fill in any social convention or technical gadget prolific in London or Los Angeles,*]" serves to justify hollow Millennium Development Goals while few, if any, actually take the time to see the moral and social atrophy associated with the missing technical gadget.

For years I sponsored trips to take affluent teenagers (and occasionally, their parents) from the Northeast US to Mexico or Honduras to build sturdy cinderblock houses in slums built next to NAFTA-created abject poverty. Invariably, 'absent' was the first thing that kids saw on arrival. "They don't have…" was the chorus of voices during the first 24 hours of muddy or dusty roads. On every trip, the third day seemed to represent a tipping point. Usually at dinnertime on the evening of the third day, someone would make the observation that "they" seemed happy despite their apparent lack. In short order, the spark of awareness would light up a conversation about how *Miguel* or *Rosalita* were so much happier without their iPhone, Gameboy, or TV and their parents were so generous in sharing their lunch of handmade tortillas or empanadas. By the fourth day, kids would ask if it was OK to bring the community to dinner and by Saturday evening, our group of 20 youth would expand to a cookout for 150 members of the community. Food, singing, dancing, summer romances all marked a transformation when "they" became "us". By Sunday morning's departure, tears, photos, promises of 'never forgetting' would flow as freely as the trash filled gutters in the muddy streets.

I didn't sponsor these trips to 'help' the 'poor'. I sponsored them to expand the aperture of awareness on the part of the perspective-impoverished privilege I saw living in Central Virginia. The notion that products

1. https://www.refworld.org/docid/49b92b279.html
2. https://af.reuters.com/article/metalsNews/idAFN1E79O15M20111025

begin at *Best Buy* or on-line at *Amazon* led to willful ignorance about the lives lived by people at the source of materials or products. By bridging these worlds, a tiny ember of interconnection was lit and, in many instances, placed a global awareness inextricably and irritatingly into young people who entered a place-agnostic community.

How do insect appearances, tiger stripes and teenagers in Reynosa, Mexico relate? For me the connection is crystal clear. *Our prevailing narrative places 'dominion' in the hands of those who define the 'needs' of others.* This story is born of the deeper story of separation. When did who decide that gold and copper were to be taken at all costs—both human and environmental? What was the 'developmental' mandate that said liquids had to be served in single use plastic bottles derived from extracted oil? All of these examples are born of separation and its cousin—mobility. Detach a person from place and suddenly you 'need' your diet Coke for the road. You 'need' to 'stay connected' with phones and computers because you're *not connected*.

I've yet to meet *communities of persistence* (the term I use instead of the pejorative term 'indigenous') that elect isolation over community gatherings. And I've yet to sit in social interactions within those communities without feeling like they're devoid of a sense of urgency and agenda. Gatherings can go on for hours with no clear beginning, no clear purpose, and no clear conclusion yet when completed, somehow what happens 'next' is known by everyone. Like flocking birds swooping in unison or schooling fish flashing in an electric blue cloud of brilliance, it seems that a transient 'together' place defines not the individual but defines the collective and the individuals' roles therein. *Are we defined by place or are we defined by the conditions in which we place ourselves?*

Which seems to beg a fundamental question.

Do we 'live' by imposition—placing our perspectives and needs *on* our physical and social ecosystem—or do we 'live' by participating *in* our ecosystem?

Do we camouflage to compete for scarce resources, or do we allow the environment to inform and transform our living?

In the mid-1990s, I was a professor at the University of Virginia. One of my roles was to link university research capabilities with industrial applications. And in what would become much of my next three decades of effort, this journey included an acquaintance with insurance magnate Maurice 'Hank' Greenberg. Hank was the CEO of AIG—one of the world's most powerful financial institutions and commanded respect from industries of all sorts. One morning, Hank was hosting a meeting on the future of healthcare and its implications on AIG's business and asked me to come to New York.

"Head to the airport where you'll have a ticket waiting at the US Airways counter," I was told by Hank's colleague Mitch.

I had gone to work that morning dressed for UVA activities, not in a suit. I was wearing a green double-breasted jacket, a white shirt with my signature bowtie, khaki slacks and brown shoes. I quickly shoved my notebook into my briefcase and headed up to the Charlottesville Albemarle airport. As promised, I had a ticket and boarded the plane.

Arriving a few hours later in La Guardia, I hopped in a cab and headed towards 70 Pine St. Entering the building, I was struck by the absence of anyone in the cavernous hallway that is ornately appointed with gold veneer and art deco lighting. Turning to the left bank of elevators, I pressed the button and awaited the next lift. A few seconds later, the elevator door opened to reveal a man, considerably older than me wearing a green double-breasted jacket, a white shirt and bowtie, khaki slacks and browns shoes. He and I exchanged glances for a few seconds with the incredulity of our mirrored appearance. My perplexed expression melted as I saw *another* man in the elevator dressed exactly the same way pushing a janitor's cart. In an instant, I realized that, quite by accident, I had dressed as the cleaning staff for 70 Pine St—an observation that was the butt of several sarcastic jokes for the rest of my day with AIG's leadership. I was the stick insect on the tree, the tiger in the brush, the chameleon in the jungle... I was the cleaner. And what I noticed in this experience is that my literal attire shaped the interaction I had. People for whom my appearance defined 'janitor' retained a consciousness of this similarity throughout our day's interactions. Could I be taken seriously when discussing electromagnetic technologies—both diagnostic and therapeutic—when I looked like the garbage collector?

Whether it's dress, custom, skin color, accent, language, cosmology or any other place-associated feature, *from* is more often than not an implicit distinction leading to the notion of the *separate other*. And even when traditional dress or novel expression is celebrated, its accommodation is often viewed as implicit to a hierarchy of 'development' or 'superiority'. These hierarchies, born of myths of division and competition, blind us to the wealth of pluralistic perspective and prevent us from the subtle total environmental awareness that can allow us to effortlessly thrive in the 'where' we find ourselves.

You are not *where you're from*. And importantly, neither is anyone else. Your environment shapes your language, your myths and social values, your diet, your immunology, and your ambient awareness, to be sure. But the degree to which you take this on as identity rather than a conscious perspective that informs your appreciation of the plurality of the experience of others is up to you. And your willingness to assimilate the wealth of nations (not Adam Smith's, but the wealth of shared perspective) is an indicator of who you are and who you will become.

IV

You Are What Your Parents Were

Ahmedabad is a sweltering hot place in the State of Gujarat in India's western extreme. Bordering Pakistan, it has enjoyed the dubious distinction of being a flash point for Hindu and Muslim racial tensions for many years. I was invited to the Indian Institute for Management in Ahmedabad in 2002 during the height of the most recent bloody and deadly riots. With about 14% of its population Muslim, this predominantly Hindu state has seen ambient violence between communities boil over into mass casualties in 1969 and 2002 most dramatically. Prime Minister of India Narendra Damodardas Modi was the Chief Minister of Gujarat during the riots. His political career has been a case-study in the use of ancestral identity to mobilize a Hindu majority into his tidal wave of political fortune despite questions of how he handled the riots that welcomed me to India.

When Professor Anil Gupta first invited me to lecture at IIM-A, my knowledge of India and its caste system was functionally non-existent. This in no way suggests that I had not studied it, and Hinduism, with great fascination. But the truth is that, like so many other cultural nuances, the cosmology that underpins the caste system cannot be learned. It must be lived. And it must be lived for generations. Over the din of Hindu temple occupants banging on pots and pans to interrupt the calls to prayer emanating from the minarets that dot Ahmedabad's skyline, I will always remember the conversations I had with Anil and several of his students on the concept of inter-caste marriage during my first visit.

Please understand that I'm doing a great injustice to complexity of the Hindu principles in the summary that I'm presenting. But indulge me as it makes an interesting point. In the pursuit of dharma or the completion of life's purpose, Hindu text states that Lord Krishna 'created' humanity with four classes of people[1]—the Brahman (priests and teachers), the Kshatriyas (warriors and rulers), Vaishyas (farmers, merchants and traders), Shudras (laborers)—with the additional unclassified Dalits (or outcasts) for whom menial tasks of basic municipal hygiene serve as their only function. While convention (and politics) describes these classifications largely by birth from arranged (or hybridized) marriage, some scholars argue that the assignment to caste is a function of your thoughts. You can be tamasic in which you are dull-witted and lazy of mind for which hard labor is your only suitable use. You can be rajasic and thus be drawn to money, power, and status making you suitable to be a warrior, politician or businessperson. Finally, you can be sattvic in which case you are suited to noble thinking, contemplation, and teaching. The reliance on birth, *guna* (aptitude), or *karma* (function) varies from community to community.

While all around us Hindus were bludgeoning Muslims to death and Muslims were setting fire to buildings occupied by Hindus, I was trying to understand how 'modern, educated' students could so completely embrace caste racism, elitism, and open ethnic hostility. In the eighteen years since, I've concluded that deeper inquiry only serves to heighten the mystery. But the more I listened, the more the mists seemed to resolve in part. Students at the most prestigious business school in the world were gladly participating in arranged marriages within their castes, selecting their wedding dates by astrological charts and confidently stating that they 'knew' that their parents were entirely capable of making decisions that would impact decades to come.

To the Occidental value system, self-determination is paramount. You are what you make of yourself. Now we know this is a crock of shit

---

1. *Bhagavad Gita* IV:13.

64

but aspirationally we want it to be true. The students to whom I was speaking were participating *in* a much larger atemporal cosmology. Instead of marrying rightly to beget rightly, they were describing a system in which their union with another would predispose the incarnation of an offspring that was more likely to improve their *guna* and *karma*. Brahman to Brahman weddings weren't for the purpose of creating a Brahman child—though that was certainly the desire. Rather it was to increase the probability of an environment into which thoughts and deeds would manifest ideal functions. Put another way, procreation was *not about racial redundancy* but rather the establishing of a field of possibility into which 'elevated' expressions of humanity could emerge. As hard as I tried, I struggled to see the nuance of worldview that so clearly 'put people in their place' and, to make matters worse, encouraged the destitute to embrace their lot and do nothing to transform it.

There's no question that a huge number of Dalits live without sanitation, adequate nutrition, and basic respect. Beggars on the street are often treated with greater contempt and derision than that afforded to dogs, elephants, camels and cows. In the 21st century, the 'sub-human' abuse of these communities and people is reminiscent of the racial oppression during the founding of the United States during which blacks were designated as three-fifths human. The Brahman that beats his housekeeper and the police officer in St. Louis that shoots an unarmed black youth are the consequence of these 'belief' systems at their extreme and neither can be justified nor accommodated. Notwithstanding the abuses, a worldview that embraces procreation as a future potential expression of an 'improved' condition is not unique to India and persists well beyond Hinduism.

Let's take a look at our current model of procreation. Based on our current narrative, a man's sperm and woman's egg unite after about 100 million sperm cells enter the fallopian Olympics. Philo of Alexandria—a Jewish philosopher living in Alexandria, Egypt during the change of the BC clock—described *Logos spermatikos* as man's reason and virtue uniting with the mother's soul.[2] For centuries before and after the big clock reset, obsession over reproductive fluids attracted considerable attention. From oral sex and the drinking of semen to the promotion of sexual maturation or virility, to ritualistic Eucharist, the utility of semen has enjoyed wide-ranging extra-procreative value.[3] Sir Mansfield George Smith-Cumming reportedly advocated the use of semen for invisible ink as it is known to fluoresce under ultra-violet light for communications within the British Secret Service.

As their reproductive anatomy and dynamics are more hidden, far less consideration was (and is) given to the ovulation and fertilization subtleties of women. The 'mystery' of procreation has been associated with excessively male dominated narrative around the process of fertilization and proliferation, but classic literature suggests that this was not always the case.

In the *Epic of Gilgamesh* a very different masculine and feminine sexual narrative appears. If our current translations of these Mesopotamian poems are correct, it would appear that *gregarious and sexually powerful women dominated the selection and empowerment of consequential men*. Specifically, at the beginning of the story, for a period of one week, Enkidu—a young man—is selected by Shamhat—a sexual temple master—to learn civilization by being trained to be a great love-maker. The dynamic of sexual union for civilization—not procreation—is a hallmark of this story. Throughout the epic tale, we encounter numerous women who—through their sexual union with men—assess men's fitness to be leaders, kings, or worthy of merit.[4]

It's important to realize that our biology textbook version of reproduction focuses exclusively on the cellular, chemical and the chromosomal. The notion that this, in isolation, is the nature of procreation is a selective story that, while containing observable phenomenon, avoids others. At this point, I would encourage you to put down your book and

2. *Trans.* GRS Mead. *Thrice Greatest Hermes: Studies in Hellenistic Theosophy and Gnosis.* London. 1906.
3. Epiphanius of Salamis. *The Panarion.* CE 374.
4. George Smith. *The Chaldaean Account of Genesis.* London. 1880.

pull up a YouTube video on mitosis. While we discuss in abstractions the way the genetic information of the sperm and egg associate to commence cell division in the embryo, we seem to ignore the 'magnetic' appearance of how the chromosomes first organize and then duplicate when going through mitosis.[5]

The reason for my focus on this phenomenon is because I suspect cultures that paid attention to procreative auspiciousness knew that energies from across the universe played a role in the alignment of energies that put each organism into being. Far more complex than today's astrologers, the precision with which cultures ranging from Zoroastrian to the modern Hindu selected precise times for conception (not birth), suggests that beyond simply your parent's genetic information, you may be heavily influenced by the universal energetic fields that aligned your first cell reproduction.

In Plato's *Republic*, humans are described as the temporary conjunction of 'soul' and the elements (air, water, fire, earth) which associate for a time and then dissociate. While the 'soul' has been the subject of countless debates across millennia, I like to think of this in a simple energetic cartoon.

Some of you will remember radios with dials. I know, I'm dating myself, but you can look them up if you're struggling here. There are pictures of them online. When you sat down around the radio in the evening to listen to the news, you turned a dial on the frequency modulated (FM) or the amplitude modulated (AM) tuner. In the FM signal, information is packed into the varied frequency of the broadcasted energy while in AM, the information is delivered in varying the actual strength of the waveform. When you selected a station in the AM, you were likely to pick up a lot of static as the receiver was "listening" to signal based on a particular frequency but, as the amplitude grew and shrank, interference could come in. In contrast, FM stations were much clearer as they distributed power within their frequency bands more completely. Now, when you turned your receiver to FM 88.1 (frequently where the news lived) you

5. https://www.youtube.com/watch?v=L61Gp_d7evo

were not cancelling all the other broadcast frequencies. When you were sufficiently depressed with the day's news, you could turn the dial to FM 101.7 which was playing top 40 music. And when you were sufficiently bored with the monotony of pop music, you could dial in classical 103.5 and drift off to sleep. The placement of your dial determined the signal you heard. Your selection didn't turn on or turn off the broadcast.

Similarly, when we have conductive chromosomal coils that line themselves up on what appear to be magnetic axis, what we don't discuss is the radio frequencies our cells are "hearing". We don't have an inquiry into the degree to which or current indifference to astronomical signals may or may not impact the 'nature vs. nurture' debate we have when it comes to our lived experience. Hold that thought because I'm going to come back to it in a minute.

Francis Galton, a cousin of Charles Darwin was taken by the concept of eugenics—the selective breeding of a population to 'improve' it. It comes as little surprise that, like Darwin, Galton figured that heritable characteristics were largely the domain of genetic information passing across generations with much of a person's capacity to act and think directly influenced by their genetic forebearers. This position was placed in contrast to John Locke's 1690 thesis that the organism is *tabula rasa* (or a blank slate) and can be shaped into anything or anyone by the environment in which they mature. I like to think of Galton and Darwin as FM to Locke's AM. How do I make that association? Well, simple. In the case of Galton and Darwin, the bands of variables are set, and the signal of life is merely the expression of pulses within a fixed range (your precise expression of your species). In the case of Locke, your amplitude of experience shapes that which you are to become. In both of these schools, along with their more recent adherents, the nature of the discourse is centered around a rather nuclear argument—parental genes vs. enculturation. But missing from these discussions is an equally viable and expanded conversation about the field effect (both epigenetic and cosmic) of quantum entangled 'livingness'.

For several centuries, we've observed explicit eugenics and extermination impulses for the purposes of social engineering. Public executions—stonings, burnings and torture done to deter heretical or aberrant behavior—are as much a feature of extremist despotism now as they were in Medieval periods. The 'witch'—defined as a woman with differentiated power or perception; the heretic—defined as the person who threatened the established order; the deviant—defined as the person who enacted behaviors that threatened dominant mores all were explicitly and publicly punished to ensure not only their punishment but to serve as a visceral deterrent to those who might consider challenging status quo.

While we've considered genomic propagation through a hardcoded data perspective, plasticity and mutagenicity (the numerous ways we experience variance within our own and our genetic life cycle) are only recently gaining more thoughtful consideration. In a recent study, stress-induced genomic instability—either the suppression of genetic expression or the mutation in the genome—is clearly evidenced in a variety of conditions. [6] Could it be that the stress from watching public executions, torture, or today's normalization of graphic violence actually alters our genetic expression? Is it possible that millions of people can chant for the death of those they don't know because we've altered our humanity to express a more violent form of us? Did the Romans observe that when Mars was in a particular orientation in the sky, children conceived under that sign were more prone to war? Please understand, I'm not posing an alternative worldview. Rather, I'm posing a perspectival question that could inform a more conscious approach to our notions of the edge of natural and social influences. Far from a deterministic model, I'm suggesting that we may be willfully blinding ourselves to factors that might influence both who we are and what we beget.

Take a simple thought experiment that was inspired by some of my readings of Zoroaster traditions. You're familiar with your horoscope—the astrological sign calculated around the time of your birth. From your

---

6. Galhardo, RS., et al. *Mutation as a Stress Response and the Regulation of Evolvability. Crit Rev Biochem Mol Bio.* 2007 Sep-Oct; 42(5): 399–435.

birthday, subtract 280 days to figure out your conception horoscope. See the difference in the signs when you began your incarnation vs. when you decided to breathe on your own. These are, by their very nature, two exceptionally different energies. Now, work with someone who is an expert or do a simple on-line compatibility test between your two signs as though you are the two signs, not the one. Have a look to see how many of your inner challenges emerge from the comparison of these two inputs.

This is a very simple thought experiment using a perspectival shift that informs another view of the nature of what constitutes 'your parents'. You may be a product of more than the two life frequencies that conveyed your genetic heritable attributes. You may be that, plus the radio frequencies or other energies from a much more expansive system, into which you find yourself an integral and inextricable part.

I have been fortunate to play the role of 'father' to three children—two that were conceived and born with my direct involvement and one that wonderfully entered my life during her 10th year. From the moment of the first birth to which I was a participating witness, I became acutely aware of my role not as the archetypal 'parent' but rather as a steward of a distinct being conceived of a multiplicity of energies. While there were attributes of my 'father' role models that I warmly embraced, there were also many behaviors that I swore I would never replicate. Three children later, I've amplified on the good and exterminated what I found detrimental.

Now with these individuals well along the path of their own adult experience, I see the effects of behaviors that I manifest that aided and harmed their development. At no point did I seek to shape what any of them would become in a social or career sense. What I sought to manifest was an environment in which they could find and embrace that which would bring them greatest satisfaction. What I have witnessed in my relationships with the two mothers with whom I've shared this experience is that, as with me, they have their own unique journeys of life that are unfolding. There is not a uniform 'family' that somehow exists in an idealized abstraction. Rather, there is a conscious effort to authentically live—both the challenges and the bliss—and model in each of these a respectful engagement and a reverence for life.

When I first began working with Pacific Island and South American communities, I found their use of familial titles quite puzzling. Without any apparent association, an older man or woman was 'mama' or 'papa' (or grand of the same), people of approximately a similar age were 'auntie', 'uncle', 'brother', or 'sister', and kids were universally kids. Beyond the terminology, the behavior matched the language. Meals were a revolving door of 'family' which could variously be ten kids and three adults or thirty of each.

On the island of Sava'i' out in the village of Falealupo, a 'grandfather' had the role of putting *all* the kids to sleep. They'd be tearing around like over sugared hooligans and then, with a mysterious tap on the sole of their feet, they'd fall into a near coma slumber not to awaken until the morning. I watched to see if I could learn the method of calming kids for future use on airplanes but could never work out what he was doing. But I digress. All of the kids knew him as 'grandfather' and all of them knew that when he came a-tapping, they were a-napping. I could never work out any relationship. Nursing mothers clearly fed each other's babies. In the time I was there, I didn't hear the possessive "my" to describe spouse, child, mother, or father. Like so many other places I've had the privilege to work, family was the interacting and interdependent community—not a procreative isolate. No discernable enclosed 'family' was observed yet relationships that transcend most lived experience of 'family' in the 'developed world' were commonplace.

Put another way, the behavior in many of these communities appeared to manifest a collective stewardship for the contribution of each member of the community without a contrived notion for competition over control of resources or advantage. What did this look like in a practical sense? In truth, whether it was traditional remedies for illness, preparation and service of food, or artistic and social expressions in a variety of gatherings, one could have easily inferred near telepathic communication efficiency as many behaviors appeared synchronistically engaged with no clear evidence of traditional communication or command and control order.

I'm not an astronomer, linguist, farmer, lawyer, or minister, like my forebearers. But, as you can appreciate from the progress you've made through this book, I'm influenced by all of them. That we 'converge' like Plato suggests into a phase of soul and elements for a moment in a heritable context may be part of the story. That the cosmic rays and electromagnetic spectra of planets, moons, stars, and galaxies shape our story is without question. If a solar flare can mess up our cellphone signal, can we really contemplate that it's not doing *something* to or with us? The sooner we realize that ours is neither a story of inherited determinism nor is it a journey of cosmic fatalism, the sooner we'll consider dancing with all the energies of the universe and engaging them in ways that fulfill our own sense of purpose.

So back to the question, are you what your parents were, I think that the preponderance of evidence would suggest a hearty maybe, partly, at best. That the form emerges from a procreative act in which they engaged. OK. That either of your parents had much to do with selecting which one of the 100 million sperm actually made it to the egg in the sugar broth we call ejaculate so that it could begin its chromosomal dance—not a prayer! And that either your dad or you mom considered the cosmic fields, earth's magnetic fields, the passage of comets or the phase of the moon when they 'got it on' would place you in rarified company to say the very least. And given our observations in the first chapter on the 14 minute long renewal cycle every atom in your body is going through, the notion that the you that came out of the womb is somehow unaffected by the trillions of replications, mutations and alterations of atomic energy that impact us at every moment is beyond the reach of credulity.

You are an unfolding present that did not have a start and does not have an end. You are energy in a form for a moment in one sense. But you are a frequency of energy that, like all other energy, is neither created nor destroyed. You merely transition through phases in a timeless, dimensionless reality. *Your nature, your nurture, and your nuanced intergalactic network all inform the 'you' that you are.*

V

You Are What You Believe

Disclaimer: I am going to examine a number of religious metaphors in this section. If, at the end, you 'change' what you 'believe' I fully intend to hunt you down and feed you to the giant caterpillar in the sky that is awaiting its beautiful butterfly wings. For obvious reasons, of course! Neither change nor belief are anything other than illusions so swapping them is not an event—just a substitution of one illusion for another. Additionally, if you take any of my observations as offensive, please know this. I am only examining the stories as they are told through alternative perspectives. If you're willing to kill for your 'faith' and 'belief' (<u>and yes, that's the heritage of every organized religion currently practiced</u>) shouldn't your beliefs be capable of withstanding a bit of scrutiny? I am not opining on any cosmic power, I'm merely opining on what happens when it is placed into dogmatic hands of observers who themselves feel entitled to impose a narrative on others.

My parents affiliated with the Mennonite tradition. My mother by choice. My father by inherited inertia. Founded by proofreader-turned-preacher Conrad Grebel, language scholar turned martyr Felix Manz, and former Catholic priest turned reformer George Bluarock, the Mennonites organized themselves into a branch of the Protestant Reformation on January 21, 1525 in Zurich Switzerland. Now infamous for their horses and buggies that dot the landscape in Pennsylvania, Ohio, Virginia and other enclaves today, this small band of academic radicals became a movement when, on a cold January 5, 1527, Felix Manz became the sects's first martyr as he was bound to a pole and drowned in the Limmat River in view of the Grossmünster church. While I was told that we were neither Catholic nor Protestant as a means to insulate us from any implication of 'together', the romance of 'unique' is more fiction than fact. Like Martin Luther—the Catholic priest who decided that the Roman Church had crossed a serious line when they reinstituted the sale of indulgences (the ability to give the church money today to get out of suffering in the afterlife) the "Swiss Brethren" (as they were called) were riding a growing wave of dissent for papal abuses that had metastasized across Christendom in the early 16th century. The empire's jurist at Luther's trial before the Diet of Worms (a council, not reference to some bizarre paleo diet craze) Johann Eck made a statement that sums up the last 2,000 years of Christianity.

"Martin,' said he, 'there is no one of the heresies which have torn the bosom of the church, which has not derived its origin from the various interpretation of the Scripture. The Bible itself is the arsenal whence each innovator has drawn his deceptive arguments.'"[1]

So just to get things straight. In the early 1500s, Luther thought that the church was wrong for selling insurance against hell's fire and for maintaining the idolatry of certain sacraments. The Mennonites thought that ecclesiastical abuses—from baptism into tax records (that's right, it wasn't about salvation, it was about birth excise tax) to papal bulls—were bullshit. Huldrych Zwingli rode the Swiss patriotism wave in Zurich to officially 'reform' Catholicism while actively suppressing all other attempts of equally minded but less politically empowered. The 11th century schism that led Roman (Catholic) and Eastern Orthodoxy to seek political and economic alliances around the Mediterranean and across Europe couldn't solidify consensus control thus giving rise to countless wars, executions, and palace intrigue from Portugal to Constantinople.

From the 4th century Council of Nicea in 325 to 1967, I was to 'believe' through all this corruption, doctrine was somehow 'right'. Johann

1. Martin Luther. *The Life of Luther Written by Himself.* Translated by William Hazlitt. London. 1904.

Eck had it right…almost. While the Bible was, in fact the arsenal of deception, he missed the fact that even the sacred text itself was the product of spin, treachery, and selective translation of stories converted from oral traditions to secondary written accounts in languages other than those in which the stories originated.

I give you this background for an important reason. Remember what I said about 'belief' in the prologue. This construct relies on unverifiability. What I find staggering is that the more ardent the belief, the less capacity one has to question any of the reported legends or their interpretations. Remember, *we cannot verify any of the facts* nor their recounting. We are asked to fiercely hold onto their selective narration at pain of death and excommunication! While Eck can appropriately indict "interpretation", he fails to critique the origins of the story as to do so would undermine that which cannot be questioned.

Allow me the following example. For the abundance of clarity please recognize that in the next three examples, I am *not* saying that the stories you've been told are wrong. I'm asking you to have the capacity to hold open the possibility that if the *exact same Biblical 'facts' were presented in the* New York Times *on Saturday (yes, this one), you would find my scenario far more likely than the 'historical narrative' we've been told is the basis of 'belief'.*

Let's propose, for the moment, that I'm a neurologist and I am reading the *New Testament* account of the murderer-turned-saint Saul. In the story[2], Saul is on a murderous rampage to round up and kill Christians in Damascus. On his journey he is 'surrounded by light' and falls to the ground. While on the ground, he 'hears a voice' asking why he's persecuting 'Jesus'. When he got up, he was blind.

With my training as a neurologist and with basic clinical observations I could immediately see this as an epileptic seizure with an occipital lobe focus. Everything about the presentation—a bright light, falling to the ground, and transient blindness—is textbook occipital seizure.[3]

---

2. The Book of Acts, Chapter 9. *The Bible.*
3. Hadjikoutis S & Sawhney I. *Occipital seizures presenting with bilateral vision loss. Neurol India.* 51:115-116. 2003.

What's more, it is extremely common for these seizures to include hallucinations which can, in some instances, be associated with exceptionally varied tonal shifts in guttural utterances (voice changes).

The fact that most of the doctrine that has sent millions to their deaths for their 'beliefs' or failures therein was born of a likely epileptic seizure is disconcerting. Given that this 'conversion' is what credentials St. Paul (as he changed his name post trauma) to dictate how to construe the teachings of a man with whom he had *no contact* would give us pause in 2019. But since it happened a long time ago in a land far far away, the construction of the events 'must' be right.

Let's take another, more troublesome one. Let's say a vascular surgeon and a pyrotechnician were sitting at a bar. You know the old joke… and a penguin walks in with the following story. This guy was beaten mercilessly, stabbed four times, one in each arm and one through both feet and then stabbed in the abdomen. He bled a lot. After several hours he was placed on a cold stone slab in a cave by a sympathetic friend named Joseph from Arimathea.

We've been told that the Chinese figured out how to mix sulfur, saltpeter (in abundance in Judea) and charcoal to form gunpowder in the 10th century. For centuries before, there are accounts of various forms of attempts at explosives that date back to the first century BC. We know that legend has it that their pursuit was an 'elixir of immortality'.

When the stone that was placed in front of the entrance to the cave was removed, there was a bright light that terrified the Roman guards posted to guard the entry.

So far, these are the facts presented to us.

If I'm a vascular surgeon, the description of the lifeless body is hypovolemic shock—something that can easily mimic death. And if I'm a pyrotechnician, the blast of light could be an experiment with explosives that, when placed behind a large stone would easily create a blast pattern resembling wings. Could the death and resurrection of Jesus neither be a death nor a resurrection? Might it be a case of hypovolemic shock and explosive technology transfer with Chinese alchemists?

Cool your jets here, folks.

Remember, I'm not saying that any of these things ARE the explanation of the story. But I'm not saying they're not. I can guarantee that dedicated adherents to the texts of the Christian scripture *would use these explanations if the same events happened today*. Since they're recorded in a book, they're from a long time ago, they're from a land far far away, and they've been passed down through countless stories and translations, the written account *must be believed*.

And the trouble with obsessing about the sanctioned piety of antiquities' gilded stories is that we probably miss the entire point of the wise person who actually tried to convey lessons on tolerance, mercy, and compassion, and replace the same with hostile zealotry.

Now in the interest of equal opportunity, let's follow the gunpowder plot to the East. Wu Cheng'en is credited with the Ming Dynasty's epic poem *Journey to the West* which recounts the pilgrimage of a Tang Dynasty priest to what is thought to be northern India to collect the teachings of the Buddha. In this story of 81 epic challenges on the journey to Thunder Monastery to collect the scrolls, the priest is aided (or distracted) by three cosmic helpers. The reason I'm drawn to Sun Wukong (the "Monkey King" and alternatively the Hindu god Hanuman) is that I've been accused in China and India of being his current incarnation given my proclivity to take on epic challenges. In *Journey*, the Monkey Awakened to Emptiness or, as I prefer, the Great Sage Equal to Heaven, goes to heaven and knocks it apart for which he spends 500 years imprisoned under a mountain from which he is released when he converts to Buddhism.

Realizing his all-powerful nature, he needs to find his equivalent of the fix-everything Swiss Army Knife. For Monkey, this is the As-You-Will-Gold-Banded-Cudgel (or AYWGBC for short). Weighing 6.7 tons (see, I was born in 1967 and the cudgel weighs that number so it must *mean* something), AYWGBC is the anchor of the Milky Way. With it,

Monkey can fly on clouds, travel to the edges of the Universe for his Five Pillars of the Universe graffiti challenge with the Buddha, and variously turn himself into his fractal essence, to escape, travel, and combat his way through his 72 transformations. When you read about the myths of the gravity defying, material altering, time bending effects of this cudgel from the heart of the Milky Way, you are reading what current science does with magnets. Is it possible that the access to understanding the universe starts with a super-conducting magnet?

At least by the time Buddha rocks up on the scene, core tenants of modern 'beliefs' get animated. Core to these is the principle of *dukkah*—the notion that life is painful and incapable of fulfillment. Trapped in samsara, the only path in living is to recognize that 'shit happens', 'life sucks', and then 'you die.' Sound familiar? Buddha's nirvana and St. Paul's heaven are attained through right view, right resolve, right speech, right conduct, right livelihood, right effort, right mindfulness and right contemplation. Have you noticed the theme? Right, right? *And 'right' is defined by, you guessed it, a remote wise person who, himself didn't write any teachings but left it to his disciples to interpret what he meant.*

And this is where I'm going to get real. Observers are *not principals*. By this I mean that just because you were there when something happened doesn't mean you saw (or understood) a thing. Just because you 'saw' something, doesn't make you capable of articulating motivation, meaning, or consequence.

Take eyewitness accounts of crimes. Seventy one percent of wrongful convictions in the United States overturned by forensic evidence were based, in part or in whole on misidentification of eyewitnesses.[4] That's right; far from missing critical facts, observers saw the wrong person! Did Jesus turn water into wine? Yes, if you read the fable in the book and you're a sommelier. No, if you're a Baptist convinced that alcohol leads to dancing, dancing leads to sex and sex that's fun is sin! It was grape juice, silly. But if observers can be prone to error with the identity of the

---

4. The Innocence Project. https://www.innocenceproject.org/eyewitness-identification-reform/

perpetrator, how can they be given absolute confidence when construing meaning or motive? You guessed it: they can't.

Worse still, observers shape their observation by their own perspective and aspiration. The first is simply a neurocognitive trick. You perceive and remember that to which you can relate. When you observe something aberrant, your tendency is to build a metaphor to explain what you didn't understand. This is dangerous when the edge of understanding is presumed to be 'miracle' or 'divine'. Aspiration is far more damaging both in the positive and negative extreme. Wish to be 'like' someone or something and you're more likely to attribute hyperbolic beatific consequence to the object of your affection or obsession. Wish to vilify someone—all they did was motivated by the dark lord. And in the final analysis, either of these extrapolations is prone to be held as immutable 'truth' when the evidence (and confirmation thereof) is the weakest.

Was the Buddha self-conscious about his opulent childhood in the face of poverty? Sure. Was his psychological trauma a 'truth' of the Universe? Hell no. Did the Hebrew and Muslim texts mandate that adulterous women should be stoned to death? Absolutely. Was this dictum delivered on tablets of stone from a deity in the sky or on a mountain? Hell no. It was made up by men who sought to subjugate women.

And the trouble is that when observers are left to tell the story, their editorial content drifts far afield from the recorded actions or teachings of those for whom they represent agency. Put another way, distance yourself from the actual actor and the observers are likely to put their own spin on the interpretation of events.

Remember, St. Paul was an epileptic (possibly) mass murderer (certainly). Probably the perfect spokesman for someone who evidenced tolerance and inclusion and advocated for non-violence? Not! When the prophet Muhammad (PBUH) reportedly endorsed the suppression of women, did anyone examine the experiences of his between 11 and 23 wives or his three sex slave concubines? The patriarchs in the Hebrew tradition variously practiced polygamy, incest, rape, and prostitution. Yet these are the inspirations for the veiling and suppression of women? What, pray tell, is adultery, when a guy can have as many wives and sex slaves as he wants? Oh, that's right, it's misogyny. What makes these questions inaccessible and unsanctioned? Because the actor and the motivation for actions were reported by observers a long time ago in a land far far away.

After the Siege of Acre in 1291, not only did the formal Crusades collapse into the pointless heap of bloodshed that would be revived by Netflix, HBO and Showtime in epic series but Jews living in Germany, Italy and France experienced increasing Christian tyranny as the equally-reviled, but less armed, enemies of Christ. Many of the German Jews moved East and settled in what is now Poland, Lithuania and Russia. In part because they didn't have my book at the time (which obviously would have *changed their beliefs*) and for other real reasons, the Ashkenazim routinely married within their own communities shunning genetic and cultural diversity in favor of maintaining 'purity'. The modern result of this behavior is that many Askenazi Jewish women have the unfortunate genetic mutation known as BRCA 1 and BRCA 2 which predisposes them to a high prevalence of fatal breast cancer. Sadly, the mortality for Ashkenazi women is associated with cancer at an earlier age and an aggressiveness of the disease that makes treatment success less likely.

In the 1990s, I was in Russia working with a group of physicians and physicists on a breast-cancer detection technology specifically designed to address the detection of breast cancer in young women. Due to the density of breast tissue, traditional mammography is of limited value and fails to detect small tumors in time to arrest the disease. Using a variety of optical technologies, we were succeeding in seeing tumors but doing a terrible job in isolating cancer from benign lesions. It was during our experiments that I remembered a lecture I had when I was getting my Masters in Physiology at Ball State University. During the lecture, Dr. Bruce Craig relayed a story about the 'mammalian dive reflex'—a phenomenon that occurs when facial nerves encounter cold water. When the trigeminal nerves (cranial nerve 5) in the face sense facial submersion and cold, they send information to the vagus nerve (cranial nerve 10) which slows heartbeat and respiration, constricts peripheral blood flow and directs blood to the heart, lung, and brains and seeks to lessen demand for oxygen by altering the carotid sensors. I had a hunch that greedy cancer cells—while they are forming into their differentiated, pathologic condition, wouldn't play nicely like the other tissue. When every other tissue would shut down its blood demand at the capillary sphincters, I assumed, tumors would continue to gobble up all the blood they could.

With this hunch, I suggested that, on one day, we'd bring previously tested women into the clinic and, while in the optical sensor, dunk their face into ice water. Lo and behold, women with tumors as small as 2 millimeters had their cancer light up like a Christmas Tree when the rest of the tissue went dark. A silent killer which had brought centuries of death to 'believers' was outed by information derived from the Antarctic Weddell seal and drowning victims. My 'hunch' pre-dated the science that substantiated it by nearly a decade.[5] And for that decade, some young women were spared prophylactic mastectomies and death. What I found amazing was the fact that *none* of the oncologists on our team thought this would work and none of the physicists had any opinion whatsoever. Certainty of belief, it seemed, was not up for questions. If you didn't have the 'belief', anything was plausible and worthy of consideration.

But Dave, I'm an atheist and my world is only resolved by science. So, nice try, but you're not speaking to me.

Cool. Did you read Chapter 1?

Let's take a look a bit deeper, shall we? Let's start with something simple like symbols—letters or numbers. Both of these were invented derived from 'belief'. When you consider an alphabet or a numeral system each of these serve as a finite set of variables to delimit potentially infinite expression. When I was young, millionaires were the inaccessi-

---

5. Weixin Lu and Alan Jay Schroit. "Vascularization of Melanoma by Mobilization and Remodeling of Preexisting Latent Vessels to Patency." *Cancer Res* February 1 2005 (65) (3) 913-918.

ble wealthy. Fifty years later, billionaires are a dime a dozen. Did any of these absolute numbers reflect any reality? Are more people wealthier? Do these numbers have objective 'meaning' or are they metaphors for "a lot"? Some of the words I've used are commonplace in your vocabulary. Others are not. Do you 'believe' something about my knowledge, my vanity, my education, my intention, based on their use? From simple symbols and glyphs to complex formulae, our use of symbols have 'literal' consequence and convey 'belief'.

When you speak with friends at a social function, do you recite (or make up) statistics? What's the motivation for doing so? Is there 'meaning' in how many car crashes result in fatalities, what the score of the Cowboys vs. Patriots game was last Sunday, or how many years you've been in a legally sanctioned relationship like marriage? Each of these precise, circumscribed statistics are born of belief. Few of them have consequence. And even when deployed, they serve to reify dogma more than they answer a matter completely. Statistics, scores, rankings, preferences all project a prioritization of reality—something is more, better, less, worse. Yet the more 'enlightened' we aspire to be, the more dogmatic we seem to be willing to cast them about.

Take the U.S. Food and Drug Administration's approval process for drugs and vaccines. Do *any* drugs or vaccines work? It turns out that many of them do if we use them or take them *whether we're actually taking a compound or placebo*. That's right, the fact of taking something, not the something, seems to have an effect.

The *belief* that you're being treated, protected or cured is as effective, in many patients, as the chemical alchemy concocted in the lab. When Ted Kaptchuk and his team at Harvard published their findings in 2010, he showed that placebos *administered without deception* (meaning that patients knew they were getting placebos) worked in over ½ their patients.[6] Ironically, their placebo data actually outperformed several of the established pharmacological interventions. And when the USFDA sets

---

6. Kaptchuk TJ, Friedlander E, Kelley JM, et al. *Placebos without deception: a randomized controlled trial in irritable bowel syndrome. PLoS One.* 2010;5(12):e15591. Published 2010 Dec 22.

statistical significance on measures of clinical outcomes at 5%, are the variables right? Are the interventions and their mechanisms understood? Are risk factors measured over long enough periods to conclude anything about safety or efficacy?

If you eat, drink, medicate, meditate, worship, or exercise, you likely can examine your behavior and, before long, find beliefs that are motivating some, most, or all, of your actions...and how you are paying for them!

My colleague David Pratt used to be the Secretary for the Majority in the U.S. Senate. His relationship with the leadership staff afforded us unusual audiences with elected officials and their staffers. During a meeting after one of my testimonies for the Senate Banking Committee, we retired to staff offices in the Dirksen Senate Office Building just off First St. NE in Washington DC. In the rambling conversation, one of the senior staffers, when confronted with a particularly thorny banking compliance issue nonchalantly stated the 'problem' could be solved with a simple ledger entry. The right delete key on the right form and...poof! Problem solved. The size of the problem was a lot of money. The ease with which the 'problem' could cease to exist was, well, not a problem. I imagined the myriads of regular citizens who struggle to make ends meet for hundreds or thousands of dollars of medical or utility bills, food, or college education. They don't have the EASY button. They don't have access to the 'ledger'. Neither do you.

When you bought your coffee from the barista with angel wings tattooed just above her low-cut jeans this morning, in addition to paying off her tattoo parlor bill, you participated in one of the most amazing 'beliefs' of our time. And when I say time, I mean that period of human existence that has been characterized with promissory notes, demand notes, representational currency and our modern debt-based money. From the Han Dynasty's *feiqian* (or Flying Cash) which tea merchants could redeem for actual coinage in provincial capitals over 100 years before the BC clock change to the Knights Templar in 1150, the notion of imprinting invaluable paper, leather, or cloth upon which statements of value could be made, transmitted and redeemed was the domain of professionals, mercenaries or merchants. The use case was simple. If one had to cart a box of gold coin around, it was heavy, prone to be stolen, and basically a nuisance. Far better to carry a note that says that the bearer of the note can demand, in gold, grain, or other physical articles of value redemption and save the logistics of hauling stuff around.

In 1930, the League of Nations ratified a convention to which 18 nations acceded that defined what was called a "bill of exchange"[7] which set out to standardize rules for global recognition of heterogeneous trans-actable value units (without which trade would be more difficult). Promissory notes[8] were treated as a bill of exchange with subtle differences in terms, interest and timing of redemption. For the 50 years leading up to this convention, various European, Asia-Pacific and American countries were trying to navigate a gold standard for currency in the wake of the U.S. Civil War and a variety of trade disputes around the world. Britain (along with South Africa and Australia) enacted the British Gold Standard Act in 1925. With the establishment of debt-denominated notes with the Federal Reserve Act in 1913 and commercial banks' conversion of Federal Reserve Notes for gold notes in 1931, the death knell for standard-based currency—the notion that paper money 'meant' something—was sounded. It would take 40 years for the rigor mortis to set in which happened on August 15, 1971 when President Nixon unilaterally ended America's last experiment with a standard-based redemption currency.

While the gold standard officially died in 1971, the notion that money was what it represented itself to be has always required 'belief'. The average peasant in the middle ages didn't have assaying technologies to confirm that gold was gold. In 1470, Galeazzo Sforza—the Milanese Duke—famously counterfeited Venetian currency in an effort to

7. Annex I, Title I, Article I. *Convention Providing a Uniform Law for Bills of Exchange and Promissory Notes*. Geneva. June 7, 1930.
8. Annex I, Title II, Article 75. *Convention Providing a Uniform Law for Bills of Exchange and Promissory Notes*. Geneva. June 7, 1930.

destabilize its government and trade. Since then Nazis have counterfeited the British Pound, Americans have counterfeited the Cuban Peso and organized crime (and other clandestine government operations) have used counterfeit as an act of war on unsuspecting victims. The U.S. Department of the Treasury estimates that about 1 in every 10,000 bills exchanged are counterfeit. There have been times when that number has been significantly higher and at those times, political and economic instability is rife. What motivates the impulse to counterfeit a nation's currency? Well it turns out that when a small fraction of counterfeit is introduced into circulation, the public not only loses 'faith' in its currency but extends that loss of faith to its government.

Pause. Pull out a piece of money from your wallet. OK, hipsters, I know that you are using Paypal and Apple Pay so, yes, go to the web, type in 'dollar', click image and you can see what I'm talking about. Under the bold "The United States of America" you will see the words, "This note is legal tender for all debts public and private". In other words, your use of the money is the ultimate belief. By using it, you believe you can access goods and services. By using it, you believe that a grocery store, a bar, a cinema, an airline, a hotel will honor it. And when you cashed your paycheck (or withdrew from your trust fund), you believed that the money you received would have utility.

And belief goes a long way to reinforce behaviors at a deep level. As of 2018, an estimated 12 billion Deutsche Marks were still in circulation 17 years after Germany adopted the euro. Germans still can (and do) use Deutsche Marks. Their official exchange rate is 1.95:1 as it was in 2001. Together with Austria, Ireland, Latvia, Lithuania and Estonia, the German people and many of their fellow Europeans retain greater belief in their pre-euro currency than they do in the eurozone.

Money, in its real and imagined uses, is a consensus belief. Which brings me to the trendiest of topics—cryptocurrencies. Talk about the supreme illusion! Anarchists, technologists, futurists, and speculators rallied like lemming rushing to the sea when, in October 2008, Satoshi Nakamoto published "*Bitcoin: A Peer-to-Peer Electronic Cash System*". With its enabling software released in 2009, along with the popular social derision of fractional reserve banking and fiat currency, bitcoin amplified the wave of anti-establishment fervor kicked off with the Global Financial Crisis of 2008. As with every belief system, an incumbent abuse (this time not papal indulgences but the next best thing, bank bailouts for collapsing credit default swaps born of speculators betting against consumers who turned their houses into ATMs in 2001…yes, the problem was *US*, not just the banks!) is met with an unconsidered 'solution' which neither correctly identified nor addressed the core issue. But as the Reformation was to the Catholic Church, so Satoshi is to the Fed. While railing against its implementation, *nothing was, or is being done* to address the unsustainable consumption built on a model in which all costs are not accounted for. That we built a consumer-industrial complex on the back of debt (housing, consumer, lifestyle, etc.) is the disease and neither dollars, nor bitcoin, nor cryptocurrency will address it. The bitcoin miner of today is no more or less a martyr or hero than were Felix Manz, Conrad Grebel, or George Blaurock. They risk their time, reputation, energy, and their very lives to swap illusions for illusions rather than asking the fundamental question: is 'faith' and 'trust' a basis for value recognition and exchange? Are stories told from dusty 'pasts' the basis for sectarian division or could we do a better job of accounting for the real cost—both environmental and social—of our actions and assumptions and, therein find a better means of recognizing and exchanging value?

Are *you* what you believe? In a technical sense, no. But do you take on the identity that is shaped by belief? Well, if you worked for a paycheck today, if you prayed or meditated, if you ate or exercised, if you medicated or supplemented, if you pursued training or sought advice, there's an outside chance that some, most, or all of your current identity has been shaped by expectations born of beliefs. And while I do not suggest that this is intrinsically good or bad, I am certain that the *absence of the consideration of the true beneficiaries of our willing and unconscious beliefs is always, ultimately harmful.*

VI

You Are What You've Learned

Here's one of those confessions that's quite awkward. I was in my 40s when it dawned on me that an award that I received in the 4th grade—a giant Hershey's chocolate bar—was a back-handed indictment on how much I sucked. And that I only figured it out in my 40s is possibly a commentary on…well, you get the point. Maybe I'm not that sharp!

At the end of my 4th grade year, I received the "Most Improved Handwriting" award! Yeah! Trumpets blaring, drums rolling, please! Unfortunately, I have retained some of my early elementary handwriting samples and, let's just say, they're abysmal. Like my epic first book in the 1st grade about the "doy and his bog" in their adventures with a "beer and a fuzzy dare"! Among the many things I didn't know about what was 'wrong' with me was that I wrote (and ate) with my left hand. The former contributed to my indifference in handwriting—me, stay in the lines? The latter resulted in major scenes at my grandparent's dining table where, "I'm not going to have a grandson that makes a table setting awkward," was my grandmother's intervention to civilize me. Good luck there! So, most improved handwriting for someone who couldn't take the time to distinguish 'd's and 'b's? That's like saying that Dengue Fever is better than Ebola. It's simply a matter of scale of just how bad it was.

One of my favorite experiences in observing children grow is the pace and scope of language acquisition. When Katie was little, I would read her poems from Shel Silverstein's *Where the Sidewalk Ends* as she got settled into bed. After I turned off the light and kissed her goodnight, I'd walk out of her room. In the pitch dark, she would hold the book, and page-appropriate, recite the poems we read.

"What are you doing, baby?" I would ask from the doorway.

"I'm reading, Daddy," would be her magical response.

A few years later, it felt like an eternity before Zach spoke. A word here and there, sure. But we were really wondering if there was a problem. Was he unable to speak? And then, seemingly out of the blue, he didn't speak a first word but unleashed a full sentence. Nearly 4 years apart in age, Katie had done Zach's speaking for him. "Zach wants a drink," replaced his need to ask for a drink. Her impulse to sense his desires and articulate them simply made Zach's use of language rather superfluous.

Language is probably one of the first things we 'learn'. If you've had children, you can observe a newborn child responding to familiar voices heard in utero. Pretty cool as a parent! While we apply the term 'learning' to motor skills like walking or feeding, these appear to be among the many things that seem to come with the nature download at birth. Across the multitude of flora and fauna, nutrition, instinct, and motility seem to be a 'given'. Flowers don't need to have someone or something open them. Newborn deer stand upon delivery. Learning in those cases has do with the selection, location, and acquisition of food and water; the suitability of terrain or habitat and the negotiation thereof; and, the role within the community to achieve communal values.

"Learning", as the term is conventionally used, is the acquisition of new or the modification of existing knowledge, skills, techniques, values or behaviors. Repetition, habituation, sensitization, conditioning and other modalities are variously employed in the process of laying down neurocognitive, autonomic, and behavioral associations and responses.

As we 'civilize' and 'mature' it's romantic to think of these processes as the 'acquisition' of knowledge and traits. However, it is equally the case that through this process, we actually shut down behaviors, practices, or expressions that do not conform to recognized schemes or norms. When we continually correct a child's 'misidentification' of a cup, for example, are we expanding their knowledge or suppressing the optionality they saw when they thought a cup could be a hat?

Or my favorite example. In education training, a common metaphor used in discussing inductive learning is that of a hot stove. The argument goes that children learn to avoid burning by experiencing an immediate (and painful) response to touching a hot surface. When this metaphor is presented, education students dutifully nod in assent. But what they don't know is that in one of my favorite places—Papua New Guinea— children and adults are taught to 'breathe with a fire' and by doing so, pick up burning logs from a fire with no tissue damage whatsoever. At its most basic, 'learning' is highly sensitive to context and is *almost always a process of narrowing perspective into consensus.*

I'm going to come back to our current models of education soon, but I'd like to take you on a bit of a tangent here. Whether it's the pyramids of Giza, the megaliths at Stonehenge in Wiltshire, the Ha'amonga Trilithon in Tonga, the Moai of Easter Island, or the great walls of Saqsaywaman in Peru, anthropologists, historians, and 'ancient alien theorists' see the evidence of the actions of others through the lens of what they've learned. The History Channel's series on *Ancient Aliens* loves to disparage previous human efforts musing "how could they have done this without our 'modern' tools." Their conclusion—ALIENS!

We don't consider that the large solar disc atop Aten of Egypt and the Sol Invictus image of Mithric traditions may have been homage to "dark matter" lenses or concentrators. We've got no idea what those really were so we call them "solar discs". Says who? Do we know that head ornamentation was for aesthetic rather than utilitarian value? Of course not! Do we consider that liquid magnets may have enabled construction technology that is beyond our current understanding of chemistry and physics? When we see stones that appear to be cut with remarkable precision, can we imagine that they were melted into position using azeotropic technology repurposed for oil clean up by Dr. William Wismann and me right now?

We don't envision the pyramids of the Maya or the towers of Babylon as tripods for optical or magnetic collectors. What makes us presume that, while we don't understand 80% of the cosmos, our forebearers didn't? While we walk around with ball caps turned backward and our pants hanging off our butts a bit too low, other cultures are depicted with elaborate cones, crowns, and regalia that could very well have been technology we simply cannot imagine. The trouble with 'learning' as we practice it today is that it is more indoctrination and myopia than it is the capacity to continuously engage and learn from the totality of all inputs.

Education, or the formalization of the process of enculturation and learning, has been as diverse as the cultural expressions of humanity. Derived from the Latin word meaning "breeding" or "bringing up", education has always been a blend of *selective perspective transmission* from one generation to the next.

In its current form, we start with a scale that's intriguing—A4 (210x297mm) if you're in the metric world or 8 ½ x 11 inch if you subscribe to the American National Standards Institute. Think about it, the very size of paper we use denotes the density of our learning, the scale of our artistic expression, and the completeness of the coverage of a topic. In the Occident, we embrace nine digits and 26 letter alphabets (up from the known 22 consonant letters of the Canaanite alphabet in use around 1050 BCE). Asian languages have upwards of 85,000 characters. Basic literacy requiring the mastery of at least 2,136 is considered the bare minimum!

Our current narrative about the formation of our alphabet comes from an assumption that alphabets came to replace hieroglyphs in some languages (Asiatic languages being a notable exception). What we actually know about these presumptions is very little. We think that the earliest character set has symbols that were largely livestock, farming, fishing, and agrarian metaphors. If they, and their cuneiform and hieroglyphs actually were launch codes for "dark matter" concentrators and later civilizations dumbed them down, we'll never know.

Let's do a little thought experiment. Go onto your Facebook page or your favorite news feed. Select fourteen lines. This is the same number of lines that exist as hieroglyphs on the Rosetta Stone. Now from that, tell me if you could explain *all language and meaning of our current civilization.* Tragically, in a certain respect, the answer may be, "Yes" which is downright disappointing. Now think about it. What we've 'learned' about a civilization that persisted for over 3,000 years relies heavily on 14 lines of text from the Rosetta Stone—at best a few hundred words. We assume that the Rosetta Stone was written flawlessly in 320 BCE and translated correctly in 1799 after being found by a French soldier *two thousand years after it was the 'news'* of King Ptolemy V Epiphanes in Memphis, Egypt.

Alternatively, let's take 14 lines of text from another King from Memphis:

Wise men say only fools rush in

But I can't help falling in love with you

Shall I stay?

Would it be a sin

If I can't help falling in love with you?

Like a river flows surely to the sea

Darling so it goes

Some things are meant to be

Take my hand, take my whole life too

For I can't help falling in love with you

Like a river flows surely to the sea

Darling so it goes

Some things are meant to be

Take my hand, take my whole life too

How about it? Would we be happy learning everything there is to know about the last 3,000 years deciphered from Elvis' *Fools Rush In*? Was the Rosetta Stone a literal translation? Was it metaphoric? We have no idea. We also don't know if a feather, serpent or scarab glyph in, let's say 2,500 BC meant the same thing as it did in 250 BC. After all, in the case of our philosophical and religious texts, we don't have a clue what Jesus said in Aramaic or what Buddha said in Magadhi Prakrit (you didn't even know that was a language, did you?).

So back to kindergarten. We start by taking our sheet of paper, drawing lines and then applying writing utensils to paper...in the lines! And what colors do we see primarily? That's right, some version of black and white. White chalk on a black chalkboard when I was growing up. Number 4 pencils (whatever that meant) on white paper. Words, words, words.

For 'art' you could have color—preferably within black and white lines! Success in education was measured by your ability to master the recognition, recall, and regurgitation of words. And when words ended, numbers began. What did you really 'learn' in school? Conformity. Stay within the lines. Use the 'right' utensil. Recite the correct answer. Oh, and relegate minimal time to art, music, dance, sport, and any other expression... but even then, for only 45 minutes.

We learn about the mysteries of our souls, our abject or 'sinful' state, the myths of beginnings, endings, and vindictive super-powers in our churches, mosques, temples and synagogues. We learn that adults are entitled to hit children even though fighting on the playground is 'wrong'. We learn that 'sex' is for 'marriage' unless a parent, a relative, a teacher, or a priest decides that you are their prey. We learn that we are supposed to shut up and listen when we hear nonsense. We learn hierarchy from the bully on the playground or the knower-of-things that has the agency of enforcing that knowing onto us. We learn the comfort of a loving caress, the empathy for those who experience misfortune. We learn indifference, understanding, tolerance, tyranny, patience, urgency, procrastination and compunction. And all of these are placed in the context of 'soft' or interpersonal skills. To amount to anything, we learn that regimented education—delivered and received in standardized formats—is prerequisite to 'success'.

This social manufacturing model designed to view 'trained labor' as the desired outcome from education is a companion to the last 400 years of industrialization. Far more persistent has been the learning-by-doing models associated with guilds and trade associations.

When one considers guild education, accession into a closed association of people organized for a particular purpose is more the aim. Cyrus the Great's account of education of the philosopher warrior in the *Cyropaedia* demonstrates the implementation of a fraternal order in which master leaders were born of intellectual and physical challenges—sparring with brains and brawn.[1] Like the Spartans that came later, matriculation into the ranks of political, military, and social leadership involved the breaking and remaking of youth into hardened elite. If you have any friend who is a doctor or medical student, ask them about their experience during residency or fellowship and their description is indistinguishable from accounts 3,000 years ago.

Wonder what gives doctor's god complexes? The same thing that motivated 300 Spartans to repel the Persians at Thermopylae and enter immortality in legend. We brutalize the few who can make it and, in so doing, give them the confidence to defy the gods as well as the odds.

From Persian soldiers, to monastic clerics, to stone masons, the guild has served a template for education and learning for millennia. In summary it involves the aspirant or initiate who seeks (or is coerced) to enter a particular endeavor. Upon entry, the apprentice is assigned menial tasks to support those within the organization. During the early going, the apprentice is habituated into activities but is furnished with little to no explanation as to the knowledge underpinning the stated task. When demonstrable evidence of capabilities emerge—often through extraor-

---

1. Xenophon. *Cyropaedia*. Athens. 370 BCE.

dinary effort beyond assigned tasks—the apprentice can advance to a craftsman. With the accession to craftsman, nascent communications of 'meaning' begin to be shared. Not just the 'what' we do but the motivations for a design, convention, action, or practice. This information is largely conveyed during the 'doing' of things. The journeyman (or in today's parlance, a travelling general contractor) is evidenced from not only exceptional execution of the craft but the capacity to teach and manage others.

And this is where the story ends for most. Occasionally, a journeyman works with a master long enough to match the master's state-of-the-art (a phrase born of this very process) and improve thereupon. Armed with practical experience, mysteries, secrets, and meaning, a master can emerge. And from the masters, the notion of the grandmaster—the Wikipedia of the profession, the all-knower—can be appointed.

While guilds as a professional and commercial framework fell from favor at the dawn of the industrial revolution (as they threatened the monied financiers and their political patrons), the education model they developed persists to this day in many fields—most visibly in medicine and the arts. The efficacy of the guild system was the express understanding of a purpose. Learning was purposeful for the task at hand. Need to build a flying buttress? Time for some geometry and physics. Need to color a stained-glass window? Chemistry. Need to deliver the ship from one continent to the other? Mathematics and astronomy. Applied learning, in contrast to abstract skill accumulation, may be why 15th century France could build cathedrals while we can only mass produce mobile homes.

Education for the sake of credentialing—also known as proficiency-based education—is explicitly a product of the industrial era. Test taking, recitation, and rote recall are vital if you are to be trusted operating heavy equipment, participating on an assembly line, or engaging in the Jack Welch era of mindless industrial output to six sigma standards. An instructor delivers a fact or set thereof. You are assessed for your ability to regurgitate it. You either 'pass' or 'fail' setting you up for 'success' or 'failure'.

And this last word 'failure' fascinates me. When it was conceived, failure was the 'running out' of something. Far from a 'lack of success', failure was a water supply, a crop, or anything that just ran out. It did something for a time and that something stopped. From that sense, it took on meaning for things that collapsed or broke. Once again, something was doing what it was normally doing or designed to do, and then it stopped. How we perverted that concept into failing to meet a capricious expectation is quite perplexing…until you see that 'failure' on a quiz or test jeopardized not *your identity*; rather, it jeopardized your role as the endless supply of compliant, trained workers. Now, we love to spin a fantastic tale around all the 'wisdom' that you can get from 'failure'. This is total BS.

The absence or perceived loss of a thing most likely means we took it for granted. It's instructive to consider the attributes of endeavor from which what's labeled as 'failure' arise. By doing so, we learn that we don't 'learn from failure' (or exams, or tests, or meaningless essays) but rather we learn from *attributes* that defy failure.

What are these? Quite simple. To have 'run out', you were *persisting* and then you ceased. You can pick it up again. Effort was being directed towards an ideal or a goal to which you were *aspiring*. You can attain or try again. With the exception of a complete absence of effort, you were *repeating* a thought, skill or task as one cannot cease that which was not attempted. The value underpinning your pursuit was to add *excellence* to the rote and mundane. The notion of excellence relies on *comparison* to a known or imagined ideal. And your objective for the thing that you were doing was to *refine* you and your ability to engage your ecosystem in a meaningful way. Our current corruption of the term 'failure', in summary, is actually a lazy denigration of great human attributes: *persistence, aspiration, repetition, excellence, comparison, and refinement*. And if our education system reinforced these attributes over issuing judgments on meaningless output, we'd run the risk of thinking and engaging more completely.

While the framework for education could be the subject of an entirely separate book, learning is a lifelong endeavor. Unfortunately, we often conclude our formal training armed with our consensus approved perspectives and don't think of learning much beyond that. After all, life, and all…right? In our frenzied "knowledge" era, we learn about scandal, political intrigue, latest fashions, curiosities and the like by carefully curated media that serves us channels of sanctioned information. Nowhere is this more evident than the blight of our times—Google. Thankfully I left the university before Google was the universal library from which all information was found. During my last year teaching, I had a student swear that a reference I had made was in error because he "couldn't find it on Google." The notion that he might walk less than ½ a kilometer to the anachronism called a library was beyond the pale. Google is to information what the Catholic Inquisition was to books and art. If the content is curated and sponsored, you'll find it. If not, sift through the ashes of a book burning as you're more likely to find what never made it to keyword auctioned economic thresholds of relevance. We make the mistake of presuming that quantity is synonymous with completeness. And we're dumber and more gullible for it.

Let's say you have some pain in your chest. You think that it will go away. Maybe it was the burrito from last night that's coming back to haunt you. A day or two later, you notice that a deep breath makes the pain worse. That night, you feel your left arm tingle a bit. At 2AM you grab your smartphone and type in your symptoms. "Chest pain", "shortness of breath", "numbness" all go into your search bar and up pops "Impending Heart Attack." Shit! I have a meeting tomorrow! But, oh my gosh, I might be having a heart attack. You don't have time to have your schedule interrupted but…*heart attack*…that sounds pretty bad. So, against your better judgment, you go to the hospital. Sensors on your chest, blood drawn and a CT scan later you get the news. You have an abnormal growth in your left lung. Immediately (and without anything being said) you know you have cancer. A few days later, you're sitting in an oncologist's office when she informs you that there's definitely a tumor and its wrapped around your subclavian artery and possibly extends to your carotid artery. Removing it is probably your only shot at surviving but the surgery is dangerous given the blood vessels involved. Do nothing and you'll probably die. Do something and you'll probably die.

It's two days until you can see the thoracic surgeon to schedule the operation. You're not sleeping so you are reading everything you can about the rare cases of this bizarre tumor. Most of the stories don't end well. By the time you see the surgeon, he reviews the case, looks at the images and shakes his head.

"I might be able to get it," he begins.

In your head you start flipping through the could haves, might haves, and what ifs.

"Let's face it," he continues, "with the pain you're in and the fact that you can't sit, lie down, or stand up, despite the odds, surgery is your only option."

A day later, you're naked on a table in a brightly lit operating room.

"Good luck," the nurse whispers as you slip into unconsciousness.

A scar, recurring chest pain and, months of pathology reports later, no official tissue culture confirmation. One lab said that they thought it was a pediatric tumor only seen in children under the age of 10. But you're in your 40's. No idea what it was. No idea if it's 'gone'. Just a mystery.

Question. What did we 'learn'? What did 'learned' physicians know?

Well, let's review. We know that Google makes a terrible physician substitute if, by physician, we expect an answer. Was it entirely worthless? Not necessarily as the drumbeat of "heart attack" motivated a reorientation of priorities. Did it convey helpful information? No. Can you still find a subclavian / carotid rapidly growing tumor by searching "chest pain"? No. Can you find the event described above anywhere on Google? Nope. So, Google didn't learn either. We know that emergency rooms act based on *habituation* rather than taking the time to consider alternatives.

We know that several unnecessary tests were performed that confirmed nothing was wrong when something was VERY wrong. We learned that an undefined lesion found on a CT scan triggered a reflex of the 'worst' outcome—cancer—when in reality, a FAR worse (and more immediately fatal) outcome was really the case. We learned that pragmatism—you'll die without the procedure and you'll probably die in the procedure—was, in the end the fuel for reckless optimism. And we learned that a surgeon at George Washington Hospital saved *my life for which I'm abundantly grateful!*

When we 'learn' we have a disease, a job promotion, an alteration in life situation, how often do we allow the acquired information to redefine "who" we are? From school through our careers, we adopt a consensus behavior of identification of 'who' by a credential. A partner leaves and you are "divorced" or "rejected". And you seek the solace of those with whom you can commiserate. You sell a company and find yourself with more cash than you know what to do with. You are a venture capitalist who, based on your windfall can dictate 'wisdom' credential only through your status. In desperation, you break a law. You're a felon. You are told you have cancer. Your life resolves around your disease. *When we credential our existence by what we learn, we cease to live.*

At its very best, learning enables us to find ever-expanding perspective to see ourselves and the world through multiple lenses to broaden our awareness. At its very worst, it blinds us to all options beyond our credentialed consensus and invokes militant opposition to anything that challenges our identity.

More insidious than this identity crisis is the formulaic manner in which it is applied. While it is credited with helping millions of people, one of the most egregious abuses of the 'learning' paradigm is the hypnotic and abusive technique of the 12-step program supporting Alcoholics Anonymous. Take a group of people who are already demonstrating addictive personalities and swap the addiction! Sounds perfectly manipulative. The opening line—tenet 1—"I am powerless over alcohol and my life is unmanageable"—is a patent lie. You *are* being brainwashed and you *are being told that you must replace one dependency for another.*

Now, please don't get me wrong. The epidemic of alcoholism is dreadful and addressing it is vital. But when Dr. Bob Smith and Bill Wilson started their movement in 1935 their genius had more to do with bringing the topic of substance abuse to light. With the nearly universally overlooked social endorsement of John D. Rockefeller, Jr.—the Prohibition activist affiliated with the teetotaler Baptist and Presbyterian churches—selling 'god' was as important as ending the consumption of liquor. "I am an alcoholic," was the beginning of the formulaic 'learned affiliation' that substituted conditions for identity. And since then, gamblers, consumers of pornography, compulsive debtors, and all manner of other social addictions have wrapped themselves in the 12-step delusion.

You may be in pain. You may be seeking a behavior or chemical to alter that condition. But identification with an anonymous 'other power' to simply replace one vice does not promote 'learning'. It merely alters a habituated behavior by trading one surrogate for another.

I find it ironic that John D. Rockefeller, Jr.—the oil and iron tycoon enriched by the literal blood (Ludlow Massacre) of his workers—is the animating patron of an organization that taught addicts to state that they were powerless. No chance that the fact that the more he could denigrate the value of humanity with squalor the more enriched he got might have been as much motivation as his objections about intemperance. Nah. After all, he used some of that hard-earned money to build buildings and art galleries that I'm sure aided the families of those he literally worked to death or had murdered.

Back to the beginning of this inquiry—what are we learning and who benefits? It's high time we take a closer look at both of these components. In a world filled with forecasts of machines and robots stealing 'our jobs' like the immigrant fearmongering of the last 100 years, is curriculum engineered in the 1930s still serving us?

Bill Gates and Paul Allen dropped out of Harvard and Washington

State University to build Microsoft. Oprah Winfrey left Tennessee State University in her second year to become a media juggernaut. Michael Dell's pre-med aspirations were abandoned at 19 to start Dell Computers. Steve Jobs couldn't last a year at Reed College before following video games to a pilgrimage in India where he got the inspiration for Apple. Mark Zuckerberg left Harvard after two years to start Facebook. Oracle's Larry Ellison dropped out of University of Illinois and University of Chicago—completing neither—when his CIA project at Ampex led to one of the greatest corporate successes in modern times. JetBlue Airways founder's learning disability made the University of Utah inaccessible to David Neeleman and he became a titan in the airlines. Henry Ford ended his academic career at 16 and built the largest business of his time. Buckminster Fuller was expelled from Harvard for "irresponsibility and lack of interest." Walt Disney left school at 16 and developed one of the world's most iconic media brands. Richard Branson, Elizabeth Holmes, Adele, Evan Williams… these and hundreds of others who have achieved unprecedented commercial success made impulsive, adolescent decisions which shape all of our lives today.

Do these social, technological, and industrial icons demonstrate the irrelevance of education? No. Do they demonstrate a fundamental challenge to incumbent models of education? Absolutely. The data is irrefutable that secondary and tertiary education offers socialization advantages at a far greater level than it equips young people to thrive in a rapidly changing environment. Those who graduate—heavily indebted in most of the G-20 through their own investment or the public subsidies upon which they rely—do earn more than those who do not. And in case you think that American for-profit education is the source of educational investment failure, Australia (which has long subsidized higher education) has a lower return on educational investment than the OECD average and lags the U.S. and the EU[2]. In a study of over 900 tertiary education providers in the U.S., nearly 1/3 of arts and humanities

2. http://theconversation.com/university-a-worthwhile-investment-for-individuals-and-society-oecd-31516

graduates were economically worse off than had they invested the same amount of money in U.S. Treasuries[3]. In short, education is not serving most of its consumers with genuine return on investment or ROI. And, employers are increasingly bearing the brunt of this social disservice— and are noticing.

Education must transform to be relevant. The student of the 21st century will not be known by professional affiliation or "proper noun" titles. Rather the paradigm for the 21st century will take inspiration from Buckminster Fuller's comment:

"I am not a thing—a noun. I seem to be a verb, an evolutionary process—an integral function of the universe."

What does this mean? We must examine the core capabilities of the fully functioning education ecosystem. As the abject failure of pundits and analysts have shown in the 2016 U.S. Presidential election, if you measure consensus assumptions, your conclusions are entirely wrong. In 2006 and 2007, I correctly described the conditions and the timing of the Global Financial Crisis in 2008[4]. Was I forecasting an outcome using predictive analytics? No. I was merely observing irrefutable documented behaviour in an occult industry and critiquing the system level convergence that was certain. From mass pandemics (the Asian bird flu and the newest rage, COVID-19) to resource shocks to social paroxysm (the Egyptian multi-coups), the "trained" and the "expert" are left agape when linear regression behaviour is punctuated by disequilibrium events. Regrettably, education's obsession with the scientific method have taught regression but have assiduously ignored its dominant fallacy that we *know* the variables that matter and we *recognize* (or even have the capacity to recognize) that which is significant.

To learn for a meaningful life, a renaissance of learning may include a reconsideration of what has served in the past amplified by contemporaneous insights. Let's examine each of these components more closely.

3. http://www.economist.com/news/united-states/21600131-too-many-degrees-are-waste-money-return-higher-education-would-be-much-better
4. Martin, David E. *"Social Contingent Liabilities and Synthetic Derivative Options"* EUPACO-2, Brussels. 15, May 2007.

Sensory Acuity: Human neural anatomy recognizes that humans have 12 cranial nerves. With the advent of the industrial revolution, our obsession in the sciences focused on 5 consensus senses of the 12 that we possess—sight, taste, touch, smell, and sound. Albeit begrudgingly, we give a modicum of assent to the notion of a sixth sense which is the unmeasured and unconsidered activity of the Vagus nerve. Over the past 30 years, technological "developments" have sought to constrain these. Sight has been reduced to the observable spectrum of visible light with the advent of fluorescence and engineered light emitting diodes failing to recognize the well-established physiological benefits of non-visible wavelengths from the sun and other light sources. Crop and industrial food production have constrained variability in taste. Social conventions, climate-controlled environments and industrial fibres have decreased the amplitude of sensory refinement. Packaging and chemical treatment of organic materials has constrained smell. And electronics have attenuated everything from music to the human voice. In short, in the virtual, digital march, we've constrained the amplitude of the already limited sensory capabilities we know we have. It's time that we be constantly engaged in applied, analog and digital experiential learning and critiquing the social implications of the virtual and the simulated.

Contextual Adaptation: In the wake of the Second World War, education was seen as a tool to rebuild the human connections strained under global conflict. Students were rapidly deployed as cultural ambassadors across the globe. These programs gave the fertile context into which President John F. Kennedy introduced programs like the Peace Corps and President Richard M. Nixon liberalized international student access to institutions of higher learning. These interventions, without which multi-lateral institutions and globalization would have been impractical, served to expose young people to a heterogenous, multi-cultural world. Expanding the aperture through which we experience the learning and application environment is an explicit component of our curriculum and pedagogical model in need of reform.

Synthesis & Critical Thinking: A short few decades years ago, Google didn't exist. If a person wanted to access information, card catalogues, libraries, and primary source experience were how critical thinking was cultivated. Today, if it can't be found on Google or on Wikipedia, it is often thought not to exist. If you are reading this document, it's likely that you've encountered several moments where, if you're a thoughtful reader, you've accessed the internet to figure out what a word means or to what I'm referring. It's equally likely that you do not know how that information was sourced, what the curation rules were for its inclusion, and what was considered but rejected as irrelevant or divergent from consensus. With the mean reversion derived from single-source information (justified under the illusion of the unrelenting expansion of "Big Data"), no thought is given towards the social engineering implications of privately curated (and excluded) content. In short, the breadth of our capacity to inquire is shrinking as a function of our digital data expansion. It's time that we explicitly re-engage with non-digital information sources—direct human interactions, storytelling, books, etc—so that the plurality of perspective can be expanded.

Values and Commerce: The motivations and justifications for our actions and our choices are acculturated in the main. Using the models of social convention, we are conditioned to answer the question "why?" persistently. Why get an education? To get a job. Why have a job? To make money. Why make money? Because you need it to live. Why do you need it to live? Because you do. Ironically, education has sought to reinforce this self-serving, self-referential model of society built on managed scarcity since its codification by Adam Smith in *The Wealth of Nations* in 1776. And with marginal exceptions like Noble Prize winner Eleanor Ostrom's work, we have not considered the beneficiaries of this model. Since the Magna Carta and the associated Charter of the Forest, we've adopted the unconsidered notion that resource dominion and distribution is the purview of the State and that extraction to consumption to extinguishment is the sanctioned model of industry. We don't have a framework in which regenerative utility can be imagined or engaged. It is time we participate in purposeful, meaningful engagement defined by community-oriented experiences and requirements with returns measured in resource utilization and replenishment, community impact, qualitative narrative development, return on effort and investment, plurality of engagement and performance optimization.

Design, Engineering & Application: When consensus power is 60Hz electricity and carbon combustion, our options for engineering are drastically diminished. Our utilization of gravity, magnetism, fluid dynamics, thermal dynamics and the like have been reduced to serving rent-based utilities and commodities. In the name of efficiency, we've diminished the matter and energy we engage to those that are sanctioned by rent extracting dominant global actors. It's time to re-examine the limitations of a single power model of animation and explicitly understand and deploy design that is optimized for minimum phase and state transformation requirements. If we need heat, use thermal sources. If we need kinetics, use kinetics. It is a matter of global resilience to decrease dependency on grid and central distribution models and by doing so we can lead the world in distributed power and resource conscription.

Global Citizenship: The Westphalian model of borders dividing people, resources, and opportunity is crumbling. Increased defense expenditures are emblematic of our lack of imagination on how to engage with a transforming world. As the last vestige of control many seek to restrict and constrain their social models and perceived comforts against what is seen as a mounting global consuming horde. It's time to be explicitly global citizens seeing 10 billion inhabitants as points of collaboration and exchange rather than seeing them as competition for scarce resources.

From this awareness, we then directly see the emergence of a new paradigm for what would have been considered "disciplines" or "core competencies". Rather than focusing on reifying existing assumptions, we could engage in mutual development integrating the six domains of functional relevance for the enterprises of the 21st century. Our explicit undertaking can be the construction of a model for education in the 21st century which will be as concerned with social, cultural and aesthetic return on investment as the last 240 years have been on the rentier's extractive ROI. By bringing other values into focus, we do not diminish established systems of value and power but enable their expansion and distribution with greater benefit.

You are not what you learned. What you have the capacity to consider may have been hobbled by oppressive forces that sought to convert your life into servitude or indenture but that does not define you. In pursuit of your true essence, you may need to confront some painful realities about the amount of your life that has been hijacked by those to whom you were unconsciously beholden but, chin up, after a bit of tears, you'll see the shackles for what they are and throw them off. Learning is an ever-unfolding expansion of perspective that never concludes with the 'right' answer. Rather, it opens up the next inquiry to deepen appreciation for living.

VII

You Are What You Produce

If you haven't already guessed, I'm not a big fan of Adam Smith nor the nearly 250 years of industrial oppression that his principles served to justify. While he is, by no means, the architect of the industrial revolution, his writings served to transform arising business trends into largely unquestioned dogma. And as we saw in the previous chapter, it's not surprising that the artifacts that we produce are used quite often to describe the 'who' we are.

We might as well start this discussion at the most generic level possible. In Chapter II we talked about the interconnection between our mitochondria and the chloroplasts in leaves on trees. Remember that sweet section of how the sun makes sugar, we eat sugar and then give leaves the ingredients to make more sugar? From the perspective of you—after all, this is what it's all about—you constantly 'produce' carbon dioxide, water, and some radical hydrogen, right?

Not so fast there pardner!! Hold up on those reins! Are you 'producing' anything at all? While we love to see the world through the millions of little 'beginnings' and 'endings', the reality is that you're not *producing* anything. You are an agent of transformation from one phase to another, yes. But you are neither creating nor destroying anything. You didn't make the ingredients for your exhalation. The leaves didn't make glucose. The sun was just shining so leave it out of this mess. We were simply co-conspirators in an energy exchange that coupled and decoupled sunlight.

That's it. If you slow down—like to sloth speed…, there you go, nice and easy—this is going to challenge everything that we think. Check this out. Am I writing a book? In a way, yes. But in another way, I am merely taking thoughts that are running around like squirrels in my head and finding a way to move those squirrels into your head through the ingenious use of words. None of the language I'm using is 'mine'. I didn't make it up. And the way in which I'm ordering letters, words, paragraphs, chapters and themes is not of my 'creation'. I'm using conventional templates that transmit an impulse from me to you. The ideas are neither mine nor yours. They're ours. In some cases, you've thought, "Yeah, I've thought that too!" In other cases, you've been irritated by my kicking one of your sacred cows. How did I know you cared about that so much? Am I some sort of wizard? No. I'm just prodding you to consider something that you've accepted without full consideration. Gotcha!

See, what I've done is used a code to activate your thoughts, your emotions, your recollections and your programming. But what you've done with what I've done is impute to it 'meaning' to you. Whether it's the same as mine requires a conversation that I'd love to have with you. Well, with most of you. The others… you know who you are!

Now go back to the question of production. It's important to think of production not as an act of creation (which never happens if anything we think we know about matter or energy is right) but an act of organization, transmission, or transformation. Might it be helpful to change our notion of *production* to the notion of *'contribution'*?

By the way, if you put the book down here never to pick it up again, you'd get a vital element of what I think we're missing as humans. Our 'creator' identity (of our lives, our destinies, our relationships, our experiences) precludes our ability to live a life at reality's scale. If we could be participants in, rather than creators of, our lives, we'd let go of most of the judgments, critiques, fears, and doubts that keep us from loving life.

If you did, however, elect to put the book down at this point, you'd miss the gratuitous sex scene that's still to come but, you wouldn't miss that much.

Speaking of gratuitous sex (and no, this isn't the scene yet), most of our social conventions state that we 'produce' off-spring. Cue Sir David Attenborough again…, "You see the baby cub gingerly stepping into the river next to her mother awaiting the…HOLY COW, there's a massive salmon in the mom's mouth. Did you see that?" Calving wildebeests, spawning seahorses, and hatching birds—all evidence of the 'production' of off-spring. As we've discussed previously, at best, we've shared the lattice upon which another life energy can organize but, production? Hardly! Reproduction is far more misleading than the more accurate term "propagation".

In classic hymns of my youth we would sing about the earth "bringing forth its bounty" around Thanksgiving season. This was probably a more appropriate metaphor as neither seed nor soil begets the crop. Rather, the dance of cosmic forces, subtle fields, trace elements all conspire with a season to organize a corn cob with its neatly compulsive rows. *That we participate in the choreography is manifestly evident. That we "produce" a damn thing is delusional.*

I'm a guy. Therefore, any claim I have to "producing off-spring" is not only a megalomaniacal illusion but warrants a swift kick under the table. For my few-minute contribution to the process that unleashed a 9-month gestation, I'm hardly entitled to a merit badge of nanofabrication of a carbon-based life form. And before all you mothers' groups in your reading circles celebrate my masculine self-awareness, you didn't 'do' much either. That you provided the oven in which the incubation happened—I'll grant. That you deserve the merit badge… *oh, someone's kicking me under the table.* OF COURSE, you all deserve it! My bad.

Now before I go any further, let me unpack my rationale for beating up on the "production", "creation", or "making" language. At its core, its egoic and false. Nothing that you've done *ever* began in a vacuum of nothingness. You may have conceptualized the image you painted, but few assembled their own paint or brushes. And even if you did, neither the wood for the handle nor the horsehair bristles came from your lumberjack or equestrian proclivities. And for the one of you that continues to go on, "Yep, I carved the wood from the tree in my paddock while chasing my horse to pull its hair out," well you get a merit badge too! And you can take your paint brush and shove it up your…well, whatever.

My point is simple. We don't make or produce anything and the callous insinuation that we do is nothing more than a pathologic god complex. Most of the time it's benign. But if you wonder where indifference to the earth and its materials, global warming, habitat reduction, and water contamination come from, it comes from assholes who think that they're the beginning of the story with what they produce.

Before you've ever done anything, there was a something from which you took.

And if you don't honor, acknowledge, replenish, and steward it wisely, you'll screw things up. Those who "produce", "create", and "make" *functionally rape the ecosystem* in which they operate assuming that they can dominate that which *cannot provide consent.* This last point is exceptionally important. And before I show you how important it is (several times, so you'll get it), I'm going to tell you a little story.

When I first met Theresa Arek, I didn't quite know what to do with this dynamo of humanity! Theresa has spent her life working to enable communities in East New Britain, Papua New Guinea to thoughtfully engage their forced integration into the global community. Working with isolated communities who have thrived for as many as 40,000 years (according to their stories), she works to help them adapt and assimilate trade and industrial models that have placed these communities at considerable existential risk in the march of what Australia and the UN dictate to be 'modernization' and 'development'. At her request, I had the great fortune of meeting, working and living with many of these wonderful people. After interrupting a gold mining venture that would have devastated the forest and water supply of one particular community, the community decided that I should have a house—M·CAM Haus. According to the elders, they went into the forest and 'asked' the trees to volunteer to be the home that they would assemble. Two trees 'volunteered', were cut into timber and were used to build a 4-room house. That house has sheltered over 20 souls since then, has withstood volcanic eruptions and earthquakes, and is—in a word—home. I was told that where those trees lived in the forest an unusual number of new trees have sprung up and the canopy of the forest is unbroken. Life, and its enjoyment, persists…and the mining effort was shut down!

In the Indian city of Agra, Mughal emperor Shah Jahan decided to build a mausoleum—the Taj Mahal—to inter the body of his *favorite* wife Mumtaz Mahal. Adjusted for inflation, this elaborate mosque and tomb cost the equivalent of $827 million dollars and involved the labor of over 22,000 artisans. The ivory white marble for the edifice was quarried from Makrana in the center of Rajasthan. In 2010, a report was published in *India Today* detailing the working conditions at Makrana. Silicosis—a painful and fatal lung disorder—is associated with the hand-cutting of Makrana marble. Reuters reported in 2007 that the monthly mortality rate at the mining site is three miners per month with an average of 30 serious injuries a month. To bury his beloved (at today's rates), the emperor merely took the lives of 756 miners who would never see his beloved nor her tomb and claimed the livelihood of nearly 8,000. While an estimated 1,000 elephants were pressed into logistical service to build this great wonder of the world, records are not kept about the working conditions for the jasper from Punjab, the turquoise from Tibet, the Lapis lazuli from Afghanistan and the thousands of embroidery, stonecutting, painting and general laborers without whom no Taj would stand. We see a pristine white, gilded construction and we think we know of the love that the emperor had for his wife. Ah, isn't that precious? But we do not hear the sound of a mining wall collapse as it crushes the legs and lives of miners below. How many widows were made in Shah Jahan's memorial to love?

Together with pyramids, palaces, bridges, aqueducts, roads, and temples, history only concerns itself with the regent doing the commissioning of the work. When Augustinian Fray Antonio del la Calancha casually reported that, "Every peso coin minted in Potosi has cost the life of ten Indians who have died in the depths of the mines," did the church that collected the same silver in its offering boxes concern itself with from whence the silver came? While President Herbert Hoover is immortalized for his public works effort for Las Vegas' water supply - Hoover Dam - do we know the drowning, blasting, rock-slide, and equipment collapse fatalities (all 96) who lost their lives to put him into the hall of acclaim? When we identify by 'production', why is it that we seem incapable of accounting for its true cost? Simple. When we start with a Beginning-by-Proclamation (by a god, king, regent, President, CEO, artist, or any other tyrant emboldened by adherents), our view of 'production' unleashes a god complex which cannot be seen to have a dependency. The 'ingredients' for whatever is to be built, commissioned, or produced are *carelessly considered to be 'free'.*

We do not have any current models to account for the 'pre-beginning' cost. What does it take to grow a tree, place oil into layers of bedrock, oxidize iron, organize elements? We neither know nor do we care. According to Adam Smith and every industrialist since, you start with 'free' raw materials. To them you add the 'cost of extraction'.

I've worked all over the world from whence 'stuff' comes. I marvel at the fact that within the decade of the 2010s, the Serious Fraud Office of the London Exchange wrote to me that corporate sponsored genocide and murder (by a company on the London Stock Exchange) was "too difficult to investigate" as the location of the offense was "inaccessible". Ironically, the metals from the mine could be sold on the commodity exchange, investors in London and around the world could be enriched by the mine, but the lives of people and the devastation to the environment—sorry—too remote to concern ourselves!

Not only are we not what we produce: the more we identify ourselves by our production identity, the more people and nature we're probably taking for granted at best and decimating at worst. And for any place that is named for, or in honor of a person, the likelihood is exceptionally high that no block was laid, nor mortar mixed, no glass or steel affixed by him, her or anyone in their immediate circle.

OK, we get the point Dave, we're pretty loosey goosey with our whole production thing but you've made your point.

Oh no I haven't.

You are who you follow.

We started producing followers probably about the time we started hunting and planting. Somewhere along the line, a great archer or spear thrower got others interested in the technique to use instruments instead of hands. You see when you're hunting a wooly mammoth or a Smilodon (my all-time favorite sabre-tooth cat), watching Bob stand at a safe distance tossing a stick with a pointy bit on the end seems far superior to watching your buddy Phil get mauled to death trying to get lunch. Now mind you, you didn't much like Phil but disemboweling by a giant cat has a way of suppressing your appetite. Long before the Pawtuxet tribe legend Tisquantum taught a European how to plant corn with fish heads as fertilizer in what he never knew would be the Massachusetts Colony, one of his forebearers was observant enough to notice that the place where they cleaned the fish for dinners in the Fall turned out the best garden corn crop the next season. From smelting bronze, to farming, to hunting, 'following' emerged as a social organization principle when someone or something elucidated a favorable pattern that others didn't observe but from which they sought benefit.

Robert Ian McDonald Dunbar, head of the Social and Evolutionary Neuroscience Research Group in the Department of Experimental Psychology at the University of Oxford, popularized the notion that the human brain favors organizations (referred by some as 'tribes' or 'clans') of a finite number of associations.[1] Suggested as the "Dunbar Number", his work and its derivatives have postulated that we have about 150 spots in our brain for our community. Exceed that number and you simply cannot engage. Within those groups, not everyone holds the same status.

---

1. Dunbar, R. *The Social Brain Hypothesis and its Implications for Social Evolution. Ann of Human Biol.* 36:562-572. 2009.

There are a variety of actors each playing out roles. But within these roles, some individuals rise in social status and take on the role of leader, master, tyrant, guru, king, queen, president, dictator, etc. These actors appear to transcend the 150-network limit. But do they? Or do they manufacture a cunning illusion of transcendence by *actually concentrating their sphere of access*? From Jesus to Hitler, somewhere between 6 to 12 'disciples' seem to be the critical mass to explode the evolutionary network limit.

I marvel at the organizational mathematics of the Roman army. As a basic organizing unit, a century was made up of about 60 - 80 soldiers. This unit size suggests that the Romans understood that to allow cognitive space for the concept of a "mission"—only half the brain can be caught up in the triviality of gossip, in-fighting, and 'personality' associated with a 150-person community. Let's review the math for any of the major campaigns that extended the reach of Roman and its influence across the planet and the millennia. Eight men per tent, ten tents per century, one centurion per century. Stay with me here. Six centuriae made up a cohort. The 'first cohort' (made up of 420 infantry) was the elite fighting unit comprised of six centurions of great distinction. A legion consisted of 10 cohorts. And the legion consisted of 11 officers all under the Emperor's ultimate command:

Aquilifer—the legion's standard-bearer;

Signifer—the chief financial officer and head of HR;

Optio—the second in command to the Centurion;

Tesserarius—Commander of the Guard;

Cornicen—the chief horn blower and signal operator;

Imaginifer—the standard-bearer of the Emperor's image;

Primus Pilus—the commander of the First Cohort;

Tribunus Angusticlavious—tribune for the equestrian mounted cavalry;

Praefectus Castrorum—Camp Commandant;

Tribunus Laticlavius—the tribune of the Roman Senate; and,

Legatus Legionis—the Commander of the Legion.

These 11 roles commanded an expeditionary force of 6,000 men who, in its day, were unrivaled in most of the world. Throughout the ranks, ripping pages from Cyrus the Great and the Greeks and Spartans before, 'mission' involved absolute fidelity as disciples. Before this term took on its religious overtones, the Roman use of the word simply meant 'learner'. But the idea that you were just wandering about 'learning' was not the case. You attached yourself to someone or something of consequence and, in so doing, became part of movement, mission, group, or association. But more importantly, I would suggest that what made this work was the illusion formed by a group that appeared to defy the norm of human endeavor. By having a smaller than expected number of people command the allegiance and lives of so many, the mystique of an identity worthy of admiration, respect and fear was a natural consequence. And by elevating the *inaccessibility of the few*, their effect took on mythical proportions. Before the Romans, kings and great leaders typically marched with their military campaigns. The Roman Emperors could command from afar with their legions doing their bidding under their insignia.

While we're on this topic, let's consider the social technologies that made this effective. By forcing youth into rigorous conformity, by attiring them in a uniform, by building contrived cohabitation units, and by placing these groups variously in peril and instability, a particular bond was *manufactured*. Leadership was capriciously bestowed—sometimes on the worthy and sometimes on the favored. 'Followership' was demanded on pain of death. And like *faith, hope, and belief,* an anonymous 'superior' was calling the plays from the sidelines—not the frontline. Sound familiar?

From today's 11-man football squad (regardless of the naming convention you use, variously soccer or gridiron) to drunken bridesmaids out on a bachelorette party, you can probably think of the titles listed for the Roman Army above and make out not only who's who but what's happening when the 'players on the field' are in the presence of the anonymous crowds. By segregating the 'elite', we manufacture an illusion of 'special'. In a world where mundane is the usual experience, we can be as excited about a football match as we are about a wedding as we are about a rock concert. In each case, we buy the 'merch' so we can look like we belong. We engage in activities dictated by an anonymous 'that's just what you do'. And we often find ourselves in adrenaline-fueled highs and lows for contrived experiences that do nothing but habituate our 'disciple' model.

Much of what we acknowledge in today's disciplines of philosophy, religion and science comes from the recollection and anecdotes provided by disciples who, by their adherence and reverence, elevate one person above others. We know of Socrates as much or more through the works of Xenophon, Plato, and Aristotle (Plato's disciple) than we do from Socrates himself. We know nothing of Jesus but for a few of his literate disciples (4-5 of the twelve). We know nothing of Gautama Buddha but for the eleven of his Mahasravakas (8 monks and three nuns).

All of this begs the question: what is it about 'making disciples' that so predictably not only produces near mythic identity but motivates adherence? And what is it that fuels hundreds, thousands and millions to perpetuate the philosophies of so few? Well, this is where the picture gets pretty dark pretty fast.

Disciples and followers are to visionaries what mirrors are to light. They curate and direct the sanctioned narrative *and actively suppress all those who take a different view.* "I was there when," is used as the credentialing justification to insist on 'right' perspective and interpretation regardless of fidelity. Like a mirror, they only reflect the wavelengths that they cannot absorb or assimilate (in other words, that which is "not like" is reflected). Disciples are prone to exaggerate the miraculous or the exceptional not because it was but because it's least accessible to them. Like a mirror, they block the transmission of light by bouncing it away from any other observer at a disparate vantage point. In short, they do not convey the essence of their master but rather that which makes their master uncommon.

Disciples cost us plurality of perspective and heterogeneity of wisdom. Rather than deeply examining the perspectives informed by an unusual and distinguished mind, our propensity is to cede to the 'expert' or the 'wise' a single dispensation and from that trap ourselves into trying to reify their 'right' perspective through all manner of effort. Our current science—you know the one that doesn't understand 80% of the Universe—cannot understand because it's addicted to the formula postulated by a wild-haired German. And far from postulating "laws", he stated in 1930,

"We see a universe marvelously arranged, obeying certain laws, but we understand the laws only dimly. Our limited minds cannot grasp the mysterious force that sways the constellations."[2]

While it's romantic to think of ourselves as adherents or disciples, regrettably this identity serves to remove from consideration the possibility that we, together with those with wisdom before us, are served when we critically synthesize and examine perspective rather than adopting dogma. If our goal is to conquer, dispossess and destroy, disciple-models are highly effective. But if you cede your life's power and purpose to 'another', you do so not only a great peril but you likely extinguish wisdom—both yours and that of others—in the process.

Now I'm going to pose a more insidious proposition. I'm pretty sure that our faux leaders today actually are *not*. I think the manipulative model of 'discipleship' is being deployed for covert purposes under the cacophony of "Leadership" conferences, classes, and enrichment programs. Far from being earned by merit, 'leadership' is the lottery winning of an insatiable appetite for followers. Think I'm wrong? Today's social media not only makes counting 'friends' (followers) an intrinsic component of its addiction. It specifically uses this data to disseminate information, distribute content, and target advertisement. Do you really

---

2. G. S. Viereck, *Glimpses of the Great* (Macauley, New York, 1930) p. 372-373.

think that Instagram thought long and hard over the selection of term "follower"? Of course not. By creating the illusion that your pictures of your dog, your food, your vacations, your reflection in a mirror are worthy of being 'followed', they appeal to the gaping hole of irrelevance that many seek to fill.

Is it possible that the model of discipleship is actually a cunning mechanism to manufacture heroes and leaders? Was the Emperor appointed because of prowess or because of his ability to be manipulated by the Senate? Is the pontifical selection process guided by a divine process or is it a horse-trading negotiation for positions of power? Is it possible that a misogynist is placed in the Oval Office of the United States so that his antics distract the masses from power plays and deals that can evade scrutiny? Does Fox News or CNN care who is in the White House when they know that their rice bowl is filled with the existence of celebrity that can in one moment be propped up only then to take the fall?

After all, if every news cycle is filled with impeachment hearings, a lot of other things—important things—are not being discussed. I'm pretty sure that if you're a fan, a party member, a fraternity or sorority member, a union member, a social media addict, church-goer (have I left anyone out?), there's a decent chance that your propensity to participate as a disciple has been hijacked and you probably don't know who you're really following anymore. And whoever contrived the 'disciple-hero' dynamic—the one to which you and others subscribe—happily knows that having manufactured the iconic symbol, by seducing the 'first followers' to build the hero narrative, and by making the icon progressively less accessible, they're covering their tracks and achieving whatever they set out to achieve without you, or anyone else, knowing.

You are what your boss says you are

I love the story of Joseph, the first-generation Israelite who was sold into slavery in Egypt by his brothers. His story is filled with fascinating perspectives largely informed by his willingness to perceive (for better and worse) and share divergent insights with others. As much as it pains me, in the interest in making my point, I'm jumping over nearly all of my favorite stories to get to the one that matters. Applying foresight derived from his interpretation of the dream of the Pharaoh in Egypt, he was made Grand Vizier of Egypt and put in charge of an intricately documented civil works project for food storage. For all intents and purposes, the story of Joseph's preparation for the seven-year famine in Egypt is the birth of feudalism and the nationalization of assets.

Genesis 47 details the opportunistic formation of a consolidation of a commodity-based monetary system in which, after depleting "all the money" of Egypt and Canaan and filling Pharaoh's coffers, Joseph instituted a labor-based system in which everyone wound up being bonded to Pharaoh. Like peasants in the Dark Ages and sharecroppers in the agrarian southern United States, your identity was linked to your ability to produce for the landed lord. Your 'livelihood' persisted as long as you delivered and if not, well, you and your family starved.

Nostalgic historians describe feudalism as a social organization dominating the landscape between the 9th and 15th centuries as though it somehow had a beginning and ending. There can be no question that the system described in Genesis 47 was entirely feudal and predated Medieval Europe by nearly 2,000 years. What seems to characterize every discussion of this system is an exchange in which the labor receives access to lands and means of survival and military defense for providing what the lord or noble dictates.

From famine in Egypt to Reconstruction after the U.S. Civil War and the sharecropping that followed, an identity defined by indenture to the production whims of an aristocratic master works when land is enclosed under property rights capriciously granted by a benefactor to a select few; means of production are controlled by the landed elite; and access to markets is manipulated at a scale beyond the access of the common person. More troubling is that in feudal arrangements, the person making decisions that affect the laborers often maintains information advantages willfully withheld from the whole community to preserve his or her influence.[3]

Pause for a moment. In your current profession or role, do you have access to and understand all of the inputs and outputs of your employer's business? Do you know every detail of every contract; all actors within the supply chain; the economic risk and reward calculus informing each decision? Probably not. And you may think that this is not very important to you because you have enough to worry about as it is. This is the trick. Whether it's feudal lords of the 10th century or corporations today, part of the social seduction that makes people 'work for a living' is an illusion created around complexity. The all-knowing or talented business leader has command of variables that cannot be understood by the rank and file. Bollocks! Your time, effort and energy are being applied to a system in which you are not fully informed. From sharecroppers to professional athletes, from doctors to dancers, the notion of *profit* or *incentive* is born of keeping some or all the critical information in the hands of the few at the expense of the many. For most businesses, the greater the profit, the more opaque the information asymmetries within the system. And the illusion of complexity? Well, like the feudal lords, the creation of the illusion of pageantry, pomp, and circumstance all serves to insinuate some gravitas to a few that is beyond the interest of the masses. From signet rings to ermine robes to chauffeured limousines, the costume has altered subtly but the energy remains the same.

What's the cost? Tragically, this one is the one we don't want to examine the most. Somewhere between our mid-teens until our mid-sixties we are relegated to allocate 93,600 hours of our life to a deal few if any of us would make if we saw an alternative. In exchange for some form of work, we elect to barter our lifeforce for a currency born of a managed ignorance which trades the value we 'produce' for a higher value for which it can be sold. As long as a sufficient incentive is maintained—enough to keep us engaged but never enough to emancipate us from the rat race— we take this deal. We 'go to work' so that we can 'make a living'. More

---

3. Hallagan, William, (1978), *Self-Selection by Contractual Choice and the Theory of Sharecropping, Bell Journal of Economics,* 9, issue 2, p. 344-354

than half of the conscious 'living' of our life is traded for the half we retain. But the half we retain is when we are young and have little agency and when we're exhausted with the passage of labor and have little vitality. Sounds like a great deal, right?

Not to worry. Before long an out-sourced foreigner, an immigrant, or a robot will take your job. Then what? This is serious business. After all physicist Stephen Hawking and tech idol Elon Musk both warned of the coming of "Artificial Intelligence" (or AI) that would be 'super-human'. I find it comically ironic that the term "robot" came from a 1920 Czechoslovakian playwright. His term outlived the existence of his country! What I find tragic is that for Hawking and Musk, their fear of a 'super-human' AI is a reflection on the reductionist view they've placed on what it means to be alive. Insofar as we conflate being a cog in an industrial wheel as what constitutes humanity, they're spot on. But if our model of humanity isn't reduced to the Czech extreme of 'forced labor' from which the term robot gains its origins, then there's nothing to fear.

You are your intellect

"Intelligence" (as opposed to wisdom, knowledge, or foresight) is one of the many 'gifts' the Greeks and Romans bestowed on humanity. Like other ephemeral concepts, the capacity for adaptive sensory integration and associated purposeful, considered action has been a scholarly fascination for a few millennia. Growing up in the 1970s in Southern California—within the erudite infection zone of Stanford University and its century-long obsession with psychometrics popularized by American psychologist Lewis Terman (1910)—I recall the elementary school fixation with measuring "intelligence" and my resulting entrance into the "Gifted" program. Between the Stanford-Binet and Wechsler tests, measured intelligence was inextricably linked to the industrial production mandate on education in the 19th and 20th centuries as well as the US and Nazi Progressivism eugenics movements. That's right, we cared about intelligence measurement to pick social winners (and their capacity to procreate) and social losers (and the forced sterilization of over 64,000 people in the US and millions across the globe). To win was to be most capable of "desired" social contribution and to lose was to fail to conform.

To measure "intelligence", white men of U.S. and European academic credentialing devised copious variations on what constituted intelligence and how best to quantify an individual's capacity to express the same. These included: ability to reason and problem solve; breadth and application of acquired knowledge; ability to manipulate numerical symbols; reading and writing aptitude; short-term recall; long-term information retrieval; visual pattern recognition and manipulation; auditory processing; cognitive processing speed with distractions; and, decision reaction time.

Out of all human capabilities, a hierarchy of "what matters" was ordained and then devices to measure aptitude towards these values served to rank humanity. Not surprisingly, this century-long eugenics indoctrination diminished our collective capacity to innovate into ever narrower fields of irrelevance. In the 19th century, we used analog systems of wind, sun, combustion, symbiotic species, gravity, and hydraulics to animate our living and industry. But with the monopolistic electrification of the turn of the 20th century, we became monoenergetically electrically dependent. When we speak of "solar", "wind" or "alternative" energy, we now mean using those devices to feed a monoenergetic (everything has to pass through electricity) grid. When we think of nourishment, we think of industrial caloric production. Forget flavor. Forget freshness. Forget fiddling in the kitchen with variety! Monsanto's billions are derived from an "intelligence" that decided that monoculture agrarian behavior was preferred over *unconsidered alternatives* because intelligence meant the solution was in chemistry and efficiency (two mandatory elements of measured intelligence).

I've experienced many forms of intelligence that evade detection by the eugenics engineers of the past and present. When I taught Euan to sail on the Indian Ocean, I relayed the reading of wind patterns on the water, airfoil dynamics of setting the sails, and reading of the tell-tales that I received from my Great Uncle John Parsons that now afforded Euan the ability to sail to all points of the compass in the open sea. I'll never forget my son Zachary's ability to perceive signals from animals allowing him to interact with everything from fluffy puppies to the most venomous snakes without concern. I live each day with my wife Kim's innate capacity to detect human motivations and behaviors and orient them for beneficial purpose. I marvel at Lorraine's capacity to engage implicit signals from people and systems and detect anomalies and remedies thereto. I marvel at Elizabeth Lindsey's wisdom heritage inquiries which demonstrate current examples of ethnographic diversity manifesting multiplicity of awareness beyond electrical and digital dependencies that transcend the capabilities of both.[4] I decipher systemic codes from photosynthesis and particle swarm dynamic signaling in birds, fish, and cellular membranes and then apply them to market dynamics on a daily basis.

When I encounter advocates for and detractors from *artificial intelligence*, I find myself first puzzling over whether any awareness of "intelligence" exists to form the context for the virtualization thereof. The mechanical automation of what human automatons do is not AI, it's merely substitution. *If a task can be automated, it probably never required "intelligence"*. It probably required habituation to reflex. And habituated reflexes are—are you ready for this?—non-cognitive functions. Whether we're prepared to admit it or not, the mono-appliance dependence on the electrical (or quantum) computer is not a hallmark of progress. When we place ever greater reliance on ever narrower bandwidths of energy or information, we place ourselves *closer to extinction*! This is NOT an intelligent proposition.

Ten years from now, is there any chance that we'll leave a social artifact that could survive an electromagnetic impulse erasure? Highly unlikely. Will our children be able to rifle through photo albums to see their first visit to the San Diego Zoo? Doubtful. And if the power goes out in any metropolitan area, what's the actual survival likelihood for most of

---

4. http://edition.cnn.com/2011/OPINION/03/20/lindsey.native.explorers/index.html

the population? You guessed it. Pretty grim.

Recently, the Australian government made their Orwellian announcement that they propose to require technology companies to either engineer or accommodate the introduction of spyware and malware into computer and communication devices sold in Australia. Failure to comply with turning over digital information, passwords, etc., will result in fines and prison time. Tragically, they're merely making overt what AT&T and Bell Labs did after Kennedy's Cuban Missile Crisis with the National Telecommunications Act in the U.S. And like the U.S. citizens who preferred the convenience of the telephone to caring about abridged civil liberties, the Australian population will shake its head for a moment knowing that this sounds wrong but then rush back to see who the *Bachelor* picks to be his soon-to-be-divorced dream date. Are we, as intelligence researchers report, getting more intelligent as James R. Flynn postulated in his 1984 study? Or is the aperture of our "intelligent" capacity aligning more closely to the eugenic conformity for which the intelligence movement was principally animated? Think about it. We know less about our food, our energy, and our obscured dependencies than at any other epoch yet we claim greater innovations and greater achievements based on our increasingly artificial intelligence.

When we decide that manipulating a few symbols for a desired effect constitutes intelligence, innovation and progress—like Monsanto's generational quest to toxify the "green revolution"—we often achieve stated outcomes. No one can suggest that Monsanto's *RoundUp*® hasn't radically increased crop production in isolated observation. But when we delimit our awareness—selectively killing the "undesirable" in favor of the monoculture—we ALWAYS create consequences. And while my social impulse suggested the modifier "unintended" in the previous sentence, I'm not so sure that the intent isn't to harm. A school groundskeeper is going to die. Glyphosate may very well be a contributing cause. But so too might be the corn syrup, soy protein, and cotton, to which he was exposed—all of which lined the pockets of Monsanto.

Until we do ALL-IN-CONSEQUENCE analysis, we're not intelligent. And the evidence would suggest that making our current state of 'intelligence' "artificial" (AI) is simply ludicrous.

Worried about AI? I'm not. I'm far more interested in working to reignite humanity—equipped with its 12 senses, its capacity to ambulate and perceive, its capacity to collaborate—and in so doing, unleash capabilities extinguished at the dawn of the assembly line.

In short, the *only production of relevance is the assembly of perspectives that can inform and enlighten.* The stuff—momentary experiential rushes, contrived relevance, and bric-a-brac—do not inform who we are. Rather it serves to mask our essence under the illusion of necessity dictated by others.

VIII
You Are <u>With</u> Whom You Associate

❧

Eve had her apple (or whatever the fruit was). My *forbidden fruits* were melon, grapes and orange. I told you that there was going to be a sultry, page-turning, *50 Shades of Gray* section... well here goes.

In the 1990s, I was making regular trips to Japan primarily working with a healthcare company based in Tokyo seeking to import their products to the U.S. I worked with a San Francisco based agent of a Japanese Trading Company. Over the course of my involvement with the healthcare company, I was introduced by the agent and by members of the Board of Directors to a number of other Japanese firms. Flights into Narita would land in the early afternoon and I would catch the Airport Limousine Bus into downtown Tokyo usually arriving in the early evening. On the night of my arrival, I would be routinely asked if I wanted to have a 'massage' arranged. The first several times, I didn't appreciate the full meaning of what was on offer until one morning, on my way to breakfast, I saw my San Francisco friend emerge from his hotel room with two young women.

"You know, I can arrange massages for you," he kindly reiterated over our breakfast of miso soup, noodles, and a variety of preparations of rice, seaweed and anonymous greens.

"I'm not sure you understand," I began, "I'm married."

"Ah, not to worry. You're married in the U.S. but not in Japan," he shot back. "That's one of the perks about being an American businessman who travels."

131

After a few years and countless trips, it became routine for my friend to introduce me in meetings as the 'strange American who remains loyal to his wife while in Japan'. What became commonplace were the looks of incredulity, the hushed 'ahs', and the other indications that this was, somehow, noteworthy. And as if to test the hypothesis, many of my evening business dinners would be arranged at lavishly exclusive geisha houses. I marveled at the ceremony involved in the service of tea, the preparation and presentation of food, the stringed instruments and dance, and the ornate, minimalist arrangements of everything from flowers to napkins. Without fail, my generous corporate host would offer companionship at the end of the evening to the assembled guests. And I would go to my room alone.

On a trip in 1997, I was asked to make a series of speeches starting in Tokyo and then proceeding down the coast towards Kobe. Stopping for speeches in Shizuoka, Nagoya, and Inuyama (my all-time favorite place in Japan), Kyoto, and Osaka, the pattern of introductions including my fidelity were met with challenges at evening festivities.

I was invited to be the guest of one of Japan's leading industrialists at a private club in Ashiya, just northeast of Kobe. And this one took thEchallenge up a notch. Upon arrival at the club, two kimono clad women were assigned to escort you to your room, get you into a dark blue yukata (kimono for men) and direct you to the bathing facility—hot water pools hewn from the volcanic rock. While careful positioning during changing could provide a modicum of discretion, the bath house was a different story. Quiet sounds of rippling and falling water were punctuated with soft tones of men and their female escorts sharing intimate exchanges. No one was having sex but few mysteries followed the men who would dismiss themselves for more private quarters.

After about an hour, we were advised that we needed to be dressed for dinner. Upon my arrival to my room, I found all of my suitcase unpacked, all my shoes polished, my suits pressed, my shirts cleaned and ironed, and—as if that wasn't enough—all my underwear hanging on clips in the closet ironed and starched! I have never worn starched underwear before (or since) but to suggest that you had pubic awareness would be an understatement. And not comfortable!

We arrived at another club—this one a bizarre blend of Arabian Nights meets Asia funk. As we entered, we were assigned a female companion. The woman assigned to me was young—probably in her mid-20s—and was told by my friend that I was the American who stayed faithful to his wife. She smiled and showed me to my table.

After the formalities of the dinner service began, in perfect English, she said, "Whatever you'd like tonight, my wish is to ensure that you have a great time."

"Thank you," I said.

And with that began a most engaging conversation. I asked her about her family and how she became a geisha. Much to my surprise, I learned that her family had actually worked very hard to have her 'chosen' to be admitted into the extensive training required to be a geisha—the shikomi, the maiko, and the geiko formalities. She asked me about my home, my family, and how I found Japan. When we retired from the table to a rather large lounge, several other girls noticed our conversation. Finding it fascinating, slowly a small group of about six women were sitting with me having a lovely conversation about our two very distinct worlds.

Then dessert came. If you haven't seen this before, I cannot begin to do justice to the precision with which each piece of fruit is prepared. Each one cut to perfect shapes. Each one laminated with a clear gelatin. It's a work of art. The platter that was brought for me was brimming with melon balls and grapes. No sooner had the fruit been set before me, the woman assigned to me picked up a delicate fork, stabbed a melon ball and raised it to my mouth. Before I knew it, I was enjoying cantaloupe for the first time in my life! She took great delight in my satisfaction and went to pick another piece of fruit.

"No," I immediately interrupted, "you don't need to feed me."

"Of course I don't," she replied. "But what brings you joy brings me joy."

Thinking fast, I replied, "Then let me feed all of you girls this fruit. After all, you probably don't have a guy feed you very often."

I might have well dropped a bolt of lightning. All six girls froze. "We can't do that," they all echoed softly.

"I thought that this was about my pleasure," I replied, watching the chess pieces of culture clatter through their minds.

And before long, I was serving all six of them the fruit that was prepared for me. Smiles became laughter and we suddenly drew the attention of the other guests and the proprietor of the club. She came over glowering with disapproval when she saw me feeding the women. Her look was priceless when, after explaining my bizarre form of enjoyment in Japanese, she harrumphed her disapproval, shook her head and walked away leaving me with my fruity harem. When the fruit ran out, I left, much to the chagrin of my host and to the bewilderment of my companions.

Eight years later, I was sitting at the state dinner hosted for me by the Ministry of Foreign Affairs in the Islamic Republic of Iran. My week in Tehran had proven to be quite successful and the dinner was the unnecessary largesse of kind hosts. Seated across the table from me was a beautiful Persian woman who frequently seemed distracted by the enigma of having an American at an Iranian state dinner. Over the dinner of kebabs, roasted vegetables, and salads of all types, the section where I was sitting seemed to be most boisterous and animated.

As dinner was winding down, I kept looking at the generous spread of fruit that served as the centerpiece for the table. What got my attention in particular was the scent of the oranges. Mind you, they still were fully within their peels, but the fragrance was legendary.

"Is this fruit for decoration or is it to be eaten?" I asked my eating companion.

"You're most welcome to it," she said with a gentle smile.

Moments later, I had the rind off the fruit and put the first section of orange in my mouth. Now, before we go any further, I'm a bit of an orange snob. You see, when I was little, we lived at 357 South San Antonio

St. in Upland, California. This had been the house for the field manager of the Upland Gold Orange Groves of that area. On the property, several citrus fruit trees remained including several navel oranges. Nothing beats going out on Christmas morning and picking a giant, fresh orange and eating it at the tree. Nothing, that is, until Tehran.

As the juice dripped off my fingers, I was lost in the magnificence of the best orange ever!

"Do you believe in the Garden of Eden?" asked the woman across the table as she reveled in my delight.

"I'm sorry, what?" I responded.

"You know that those oranges are the way God made them. They're from Shiraz—the place where your Garden of Eden was. Just like the red roses there, this is the way oranges were at the creation," she added.

"Would you like a piece?" I asked breaking off a section.

"Oh no. That wouldn't be appropriate," she replied. "Men and women cannot share food like that."

Putting my orange down, I picked up another, peeled it, and handed it to her.

"Here, then have your own," I said, handing her the orange.

She looked up and down the table. A few disapproving glances, a couple anticipating what would happen next.

She reached out, took the orange and together we ate the most sensuous, sumptuous oranges ever consumed.

Are we geisha, businessmen, or bureaucrats? Are we parents, teachers, bosses, laborers? By association, much of what we think we are is informed not by our own actions but by those expected of us by virtue of our affiliation. In the two stories above, nothing about me was interesting. I happen to love sharing food and fellowship. That can be the case at home, when I travel, with friends, or with complete strangers. I find that the sharing of meals is among my most cherished moments in life. So, the fact that I've had stories like the two above hundreds of times in dozens of countries is no surprise. What makes the stories interesting is their improbable contexts.

Let's start with the most obvious and seemingly innocuous. American. The abstraction of nationality is a manufactured social order. Its origins, while debated as being 'voluntaristic' or 'coercive', seem to universally require common elements of mercantile efficiency, infrastructure dependency, and often warfare.[1] A very small number of actors with agency arbitrarily place meaning to place and suddenly, land has a name. Nowhere was this more pervasively demonstrated than the British Honourable East India Company. Founded in 1600 (just two years before the Dutch undertaking by the similar name), the East India Companies placed the mandate to establish borders, boundaries and distinctions on locations that, in many instances, operated without any national identity. This contrivance was exceptionally important to entitle certain merchants and expeditionary efforts to lay claim to that which they didn't own but sought to dominate or confiscate. When the Thirty Years' War ended in 1648 with the Peace of Westphalia, the lines drawn on the map of Europe and its boundaries had more to do with the truce that was born of neither Catholic nor Protestant victories than it carried some social evolutionary 'meaning'. That we identify ourselves as members of a particular nationality serves no more value today than it did in the Roman Empire.

With the label of national affiliation comes certain expectations. In the case of 1990s Japan, that meant lecherous executives taking whatever they could. In the case of Tehran, that meant incredulity. Few of us routinely make a point of consciously affiliating with a national identity but the ebb and flow of nationalism can change that dramatically. While protesting the inhumanity of concentration camps in Nazi Germany, the United States had no problem confiscating the lands held by, and interring Japanese in California with impunity. Evangelicals across America can wear Trump's "Make America Great Again" hats realizing that, with his support, they're stacking courts with the conservative judges that will seek to make laws that favor their particular breed of intolerance. 'Wrap a cause in a flag' is not a metaphor!

It's unlikely that we can recall all the organizations and affiliations

---

1. Carneiro, RL. "A Theory of the Origin of the State." *Science*. 169: 733-734. 1970.

which have shaped our actions or others' perceptions of us. Upon reflection, you can remember with what group you associated in high school—the geeks, the jocks, the nerds, the popular, the emos, the druggies—but those lines seem to blur with maturity. I always found it paradoxical that I was told in sermons on Sunday that I was not to "conform to the world" but I'd look across the congregation and see all the women in dresses with head coverings, all the men in dark Puritanical suits and all the cars in the parking lot black. Conformity, it seems, was meant to distinguish good from bad but the audacity of critiquing conformity seems to be directly correlated to strict adherence to conformity—just at different scales.

We constantly project a raft of assumptions—both positive and negative—on others based on an attribute or association. As of the writing of this book, I've lost count of the number of gender identities we're supposed to recognize. And sexuality, *fuhgeddaboudit*! We can think of the cliché inclinations—boys wear blue, girls wear pink—that come with early childhood associations, but what we do as men and women is all too often deeply disturbing. The clothes we wear, our living conditions, our education, our social status all serve as clues to variously provide access or exclusion. Asians can't drive. Americans are obnoxious tourists. Australians have cool accents. Britons are sophisticated. French are aloof. From the Valley, you're tech-savvy. From Appalachia, you're destitute. The inferences we make based on geographical locations and physical appearances are innumerable...and very destructive.

When we see ourselves and our world defined by stereotypical expectations, the very nature of our engagement alters. And our susceptibility to this transformation of behavior may diminish our capacity to appreciate important nuance in our surroundings. In a world where we're looking for 'familiar' or 'similar' through favorable lenses and seeing 'unfamiliar' as somehow lesser, we are at risk of being blind to the self-evident.

I developed a program called the Heritable Innovation Trust, in which several interns and I would live with remote communities and learn from them the knowledge they chose to share with us and with the broader world. One of the principles I taught my interns prior to entering a community was non-interrogative living. Now let me unpack the word first. What concerned me greatly was that much of what we think we know comes from our compulsion to ask questions. The trouble is that when we ask a question, we're already shaping a series of conditions that will impact the answer. For example, if you're living with horse herders in the Arkhangai province in Mongolia or with coconut harvesters in Papua New Guinea, the concept of 'toilet' is not available. In the former, when you need to urinate or defecate, you wander off a suitable distance, squat on the desert sand, and expel whatever you need to expel. In the latter, you go into the woods to a particular stream which ultimately flows into a garden plot area some distance downstream. If you were to ask either community where the toilet is, you would impose upon them a sense of expectation and you wouldn't learn about the biome of the desert or the elaborate septic fertilizing systems of the forest. So I would teach my interns to engage without asking *any questions*. In other words, only observe.

One of the exercises I did with my teams was to take them to a beach. Without any preparation, I would instruct them to walk on the beach and find a shell. Dutifully, everyone would wander off returning with their shell. Sometimes colorful, sometimes spiraled, always interesting in some discrete manner. Then I would hand out a piece of paper and pencil, sit them down on the beach, and ask them to write down everything that they see in quantities exceeding two. Waves, trees, birds, sand, clouds, invariably showed up on everyone's paper. But in the decades of running the experiment, no one ever wrote down shells. Now mind you, for over 30 minutes, they'd been looking at thousands of shells. But as they were looking for 'the one', having found it, all others ceased to exist. When we get accustomed to the 'look', 'feel', or habituation of an environment or an activity, our powers of perception diminish. Get too caught up in who you are based on who you hang out with and before long, you'll forget both.

This is the trouble with identity derived from association. When we allow classifiers to describe ourselves or our awareness of others, we diminish our capacity to appreciate nuance. In neurophysiology we refer to this as neural adaption. What this means is that a repeated stimulus, over time, leads to a deadening of our sensory capacity. Live near an airport or railroad—before long you don't hear the planes or trains. Hear a fan or buzzing sound—not for long. After a short period of time, your processing of the acoustics will simply stop. The soundwaves didn't cease. You just stopped paying attention. When you embrace what you are told you are by virtue of association, you become a victim of that classification—for good or for ill.

Several years ago, I went to Lowes to buy another fruit tree for the yard. Walking through the garden center in the spring before there were any leaves on the potted sticks, I came across a Gala apple tree and bought it. Upon arriving home, I dug a hole, stuck the tree in the ground and waited. The first year, the tree sprouted leaves and a few flowers but no fruit. The next year, with the Spring came lovely white flowers with pink blush stripes at the center. Then the leaves. Then, little tiny green apples. I watched as the Summer came and as the little apples grew. It was probably around June when I started noticing that the apples were not growing in the shape of apples. They were a bit more bumpy and definitely more elongated than the average apple. By July, it was rather clear that the apples were…well, um, not apples but rather pears.

"No problem," I thought. "I love pears."

But as the Summer wore on, from time to time I'd take a look at my pears and see that they were remaining quite green and very hard. Harder than the average pear to be certain. Harder than an apple! And after apple season was in full swing, my pears were still rock hard and green. The squirrels got one or two before I finally picked them in October. Still hard. I sat them on the counter for several days. Still hard.

Finally, I cut one of the two and ate it. It tasted like pear but was hard enough that it wasn't pleasant to finish.

The next year I got a bumper crop. And before I could harvest them, a hurricane arrived late in the season. While the winds were whipping around the house shaking the tree with merciless force, I noticed the pears were falling. So, out I went into the gale and collected the fruit as it fell. I had a huge haul. In I went and, without missing a beat, got my giant pot out from beneath the stove and cut the fruit and placed it to boil. Hours later, a beautiful yellow color filled the pot. Through the colander and moments later—pear sauce.

Each time I have served the pear sauce, people rave about how good my apple sauce is. Did I make it from scratch? Did I add sugar? What's the unique flavor? See by association, my pear sauce became what the pears never were. Apples! Well that was until I served some to one of my Asian friends for whom the letter 'L' has some challenge.

"I love your apper sauce", he said.

And with that simple statement, I have an identity for my funky tree. I call it an Apper tree.

What would you call yourself if you didn't use anyone or anything else's associations to label you?

142

IX

You Are What You Consume

✦

Phytophagous. What a great word. While this word can be used to describe many animals, I happen to be using in the context of—you guessed it—caterpillars! These little beasts are fascinating for a myriad of reasons—and not because they turn into pretty butterflies! Just wait for a moment and pay attention to the phytophagous phase. No, I'm not going to stop with that word because it's too cool. To provide the nutrition required for the entire life cycle of flying goo sac (my name for the three-phase life of the egg-caterpillar-butterfly trinity), caterpillars spend between 2—4 weeks eating as much as 10,000 times their body weight. Talk about an eating disorder! Holy shit. Yes, that too. When you're eating that much, you're pooing out a lot. But you're also growing. From egg to chrysalis, it's not uncommon for a caterpillar to go through 5-6 skins and increase in mass 1,000-fold. Think you've got a problem with ice cream and cake? If you weigh less than 4 tons, you haven't outeaten a caterpillar. Now imagine if you just ate pizza. That's it. All the time, every day. To match a caterpillar, you'd need to slam down about 54,000 pizzas each day or about 2,250 per hour which works out to about 37 pizzas a minute.

What makes these crazy phytophages (that's the cool word when used as a noun) somewhat mysterious is their remarkable pickiness. You'd think that to eat that much you'd basically have to mow down everything in sight. But they don't. In fact, the caterpillar has external chemoreceptors that allow it to precisely select only those plants that are *perfect* for its nutrition.[1] Far from being indiscriminate, it only takes in what it knows will nourish it. It's primary energy requirement, as you can imagine, is to power the 248 muscles in its head to—you guessed it— EAT! And just so you don't feel too bad about the pizza thing—you know, not able to keep up with a caterpillar—the human body contain about 630 muscles of which about 50 (or 8%) are involved in eating and digestion. The cat-erpillar has 6 times as many muscles and almost all of them are for one purpose—constant eating.

Now when we kicked this book off, we talked about the whole 'you are what you eat' notion and so I'm not going to talk about eating here. Rather, I'm going to talk about consumption of ideas, stuff, and narratives. If we'd think about these as much as we prioritize putting food in our faces, we might all be a bit healthier.

I have an idea. Actually, come to think of it, I don't. Well, maybe... um, I don't know. An idea is, by definition, a representation of a thought or concept. Like so many other philosophical musings, this capacity to form thoughtful abstractions—scenarios, pictures, or sequences—has long been considered an essential 'human' feature. In Plato's *Republic* he suggests that ideas *"are intellected but not seen."*[2] Don't worry if that doesn't make sense. Together with the other abstractions that occupied his conversation—things like justice, good, power, truth and tyranny— ideas were thought to be universally available but not always perceived, integrated nor assimilated. Least of all, the notion that ideas could be 'shared' was seen as constraining the concept too much.

It's helpful to think of ideas as a dictionary or reference catalog. A certain set of observations are made and some set of them form an idea. To use a concept developed by one of my most esteemed authors Gregory Bateson, ideas seem to form within the conceptual space demarcated by points of potentially unrelated inputs. Let's have an example. Hunger can be an idea. When we are infants, we may perceive that there's a general

---

1. Schoonhoven L.M. (1987) *What Makes a Caterpillar Eat? The Sensory Code Underlying Feeding Behavior.* In: Chapman R.F., Bernays E.A., Stoffolano J.G. (eds) Perspectives in *Chemoreception and Behavior.* Proceedings in Life Sciences. Springer, New York, NY
2. Plato, *Republic* Bk. VI 507b-c

uncomfortability in our tummies. We suckle from our mother's breast for a bit and the sense goes away. She seems to know when we want to eat at the outset but at some point, we see her doing something other than feeding us when we have that feeling. We have no *idea* what could be more important than us so, we vocalize our general displeasure. A bit later, we get more milk. Once or twice and all the sudden, crying (which has nothing to do with nutrition in an absolute sense) is seen to trigger a favorable response. Before long, we start testing out the idea. Cry. Response. Cry. Response. "Hey," we think in our little heads, "maybe this crying thing might work in other situations." Poo in our diaper. Cry. Fall down and get a boo-boo. Cry. It's highly likely that our first *ideas* or notions are highly manipulative. We want our priorities addressed and we navigate strategies to get attention paid to them.

Early ideation goes hand in hand with conditional nurturing. What appear to be random actions take on responses—sometimes positive and sometimes negative. The stimuli, in and of themselves, are agnostic and have no correlated association. But in time, we find that the notion of applying a known pattern to a plausibly unknown circumstance works. Before long, we're a two-year-old! In Chapter X I'm going to address this a bit more, but I would suggest that 'ideas' are the unexplained, but expected, variance in the way our lives unfold. Whatever we're thinking, whatever notion we have, is not explicit but it is a blank that we fill in based on reasonable sets of observations.

This early process is 'our' lived experience. These are our ideas. But soon, we become aware of the ideas of others. It doesn't take long for idea-sense to impact our interactions with others. When I was walking to Citrus Elementary School in Upland California, I became aware that it was a bad idea to walk past one house on the most convenient side of the street. There was a bully in 3rd grade who lived in that house and he liked to beat kids up on their way to school. I didn't get beat up but I saw several kids who did. I didn't need to have their experience. I had no evidence to know if I would have been beaten up if I tried walking close to his house. I simply adapted my behavior to avoid the possibility.

During my Kindergarten year, my first best friend was killed in an avalanche in the San Gabriel Mountains less than 30 minutes from my home. A few years later, my next best friend was stabbed to death while practicing piano at a local school. These two events—neither in which I was involved in a direct sense—gave rise to my 'idea' that the cost of friendship was risk of great loss. As much as I have confronted that idea throughout my life, I can still, as I write, feel the childhood impulses that gave rise to one of my most persistent challenges. Some of our ideas are formed in shocks while others incubate over time. In schools, churches, social settings and families, the ideas of others bombard us constantly. Before long, we find ourselves developing complex notions like *fear, isolation, power, inadequacy, greed, happiness, sadness, futility, friendship, enemy, good, bad,* and many more. I have long held that *none* of these ideas are grounded in reality. Rather, they are programmed into existence by our dominant social narratives.

Fear, reportedly a basic instinct, isn't. Surprise maybe. But fear? We are taught and habituated into anticipating that 'next' is bad. Don't go down that dark alley! Because something's going to get you. Don't do a particular behavior! Because a vindictive god or parent might find out. And the reason for my objection to the notion that these ideas are instinctual is that our behavioral patterning defies their existence. Nearly *all of your next moments in your life have been monotonously good!* You weren't mauled by a sabre-tooth tiger like Phil; you weren't stabbed in the shower; a lightning bolt didn't strike you when you said f#ck or any other expletive; and for the most part; you were maintaining a rather mundane existence and it was working out for you. Like 'belief' discussed in the beginning of the book, ideas are abstractions that we manufacture that disrupt the evidence of persistent mostly good. Do you have a 'body image'? Not most of the time. It shows up when you encounter comparators. Are you primarily sad? Only when you distract yourself from the fact of your beating heart, breathing lungs, expansive and welcoming environment and capacity to sense and feel. Think of each of the bolded 'ideas' as a string on a 12-string guitar. If you loosen or tighten any of the strings, they sound horrible. But that's because you changed their tuning.

- The frequency that can be corrupted into <u>fear</u> is *anticipation* directed to a negative outcome.

- The frequency that can be corrupted into <u>isolation</u> is *belonging* directed to a negative outcome.

- The frequency that can be corrupted into <u>power</u> is *agency* directed to a negative outcome.

- The frequency that can be corrupted into <u>inadequacy</u> is *capability* directed to a negative outcome.

- The frequency that can be corrupted into <u>greed</u> is *sufficiency* directed to a negative outcome.

- The frequency that can be corrupted into <u>happiness</u> is *contentment* directed to a negative outcome.

- The frequency that can be corrupted into <u>sadness</u> is *gratitude* directed to a negative outcome.

- The frequency that can be corrupted into <u>futility</u> is *accomplishment* directed to a negative outcome.

- The frequency that can be corrupted into <u>friendship</u> is *community* directed to a negative outcome.

- The frequency that can be corrupted into <u>enemy</u> is *distinction* directed to a negative outcome.

- The frequency that can be corrupted into <u>good</u> or <u>bad</u> is *discernment* directed to a negative outcome.

This list could go on. But you get the point. Ideas are prognostications or judgments in abstraction. And whether you habituated from your lived experience or embraced those you observed in others, you are capable of releasing them through the simple guitar tuning metaphor above. I was challenged on this view a few years ago when I was asked if *grief* was real. My response: grief is a *Gratitude Reminder In Emotional Form*. After all, isn't what's missing something that you desired, loved, or relied upon? Isn't its absence your experience of a sense of loss *to you*? And wouldn't we all be better off if, at the first idea of grief, we expressed gratitude for the thing or person that brought such value to our lives?

Now some of you might be asking, "Dave, what's this got to do with consumption?" Thanks for asking. Remember the whole 'energy is neither created nor destroyed' line? Well, here's the deal. When you put an idea in your mind, like an antenna, it picks up broadcasts. You start seeing the things that confirm the idea. You think the world is out to get you. You find the evidence of being correct. You think that your partner is cheating on you? You obsess about the evidence. You think that your colleagues are meeting behind your back. They ARE!!! No, they're not. But you'll look for the evidence. By energizing an idea, you consume *perspectives that you manufacture,* and the energies associated therewith. And these energies actually alter you. In the short run, your adrenaline, cortisol and norepinephrine elevate stressing your adrenal glands. Your heart overworks, your blood glucose elevates, and your immune and digestive systems are suppressed. Consuming ideas is *bad for your health!* Obsessing about them is worse. And if your head's spinning right now with the paradox that I'm giving you the idea that ideas are bad, well, guess again. What I'm doing is giving you a perspective with which you can slow down—that's right, down to sloth speed—and recognize that *every idea you have had is a distraction from living with gratitude in the completeness of each moment.*

Thank god for the Shopping Channel—at least I can get my mind off my problems!

Which leads me to the next consumption behavior—the consumption of STUFF! In my living room, I have two wooden steamer trunks. Now most of you don't have any idea what these are so, again, go online and Google it if you must. Use quotes so you don't mistakenly get photographs of my 'steamed (and starched) undies' from the preceding chapter. There was a time when a trip for a family emigrating from Europe to America would comfortably fit in 3 or 4 of these. A few photos, the family silverware, wedding dishes, a few blankets and clothes, and some cooking utensils and tools. I marvel at the baggage claim at United when I see passengers collecting luggage from their week away in excess of what was the volume of earthly possessions less than one generation ago.

Apart from crazy kings, pharaohs and the odd of noble, most of us didn't define ourselves by what we had because, for much of our human story, we didn't 'have' much. From the *Magna Carta*—simultaneously tolerated and disavowed by my favorite villain Pope Innocent III—in 1215 until 1932, most of the earth's land was not subject to individual ownership. Through commons or 'improvements', we could use land and nature, but it wasn't "ours" by virtue of property rights. On the eve of the Great Depression in 1928, the Republicans promised that an election of Herbert Hoover would put "a chicken in every pot and a car in every garage." From 1929 until 1932, this fantasy was put on hold with abject poverty sweeping the nation and sending ripples around the world. But while this delusion was great fodder for political campaigns, by 1924, most of the Americans who could afford a car had one making the slogan clearly aspirational to the working class without access to the automobile. In fact, in that year, General Motors' CEO Alfred P. Sloan Jr. announced that he was developing *dynamic obsolescence*—a design concept that would seek to entice existing car owners that they must purchase the newest, next year's model.[3] In what would serve as the gospel of modern capitalism, Bernard London published a pamphlet in 1932 entitled *"Ending the Depression Through Planned Obsolescence"* in which he criticized as 'hysterical' people using things for their useful life.

In a word, people generally, in a frightened and hysterical mood, are using everything that they own longer than was

---

3. Grattan, L., *Populism's Power: Radical Grassroots Democracy in America.* Oxford University Press. January 6, 2016.

their custom before the depression. In the earlier period of prosperity, the American people did not wait until the last possible bit of use had been extracted from every commodity. They replaced old articles with new for reasons of fashion and up-to-dateness. They gave up old homes and old automobiles long before they were worn out, merely because they were obsolete. All business, transportation, and labor had adjusted themselves to the prevailing habits of the American people. Perhaps, prior to the panic, people were too extravagant; if so, they have now gone to the other extreme and have become retrenchment-mad.

People everywhere are today disobeying the law of obsolescence. They are using their old cars, their old tires, their old radios and their old clothing much longer than statisticians had expected on the basis of earlier experience.

The question before the American people is whether they want to risk their future on such continued planless, haphazard, fickle attitudes of owners of ships and shoes and sealing wax."[4]

In his advocacy for planned obsolescence, he suggested that the government should assign a "lease life" to shoes, homes, and machines after which they would be legally "dead" and required to be destroyed. It took 22 years and an advertising conference in Minneapolis in 1954 for this recommendation to become the *de facto* <u>unnatural order</u>. Brooks Stevens - the designer of iconic images like the Jeep grille, the Harley-Davidson motorcycle, the Oscar Mayer Wienermobile to sell hot dogs, lawn mowers, toasters, camper vans and all things consumable - became the design and advertising messiah to the industrial impulse to define identity by what we buy.

His effect is evident in countless standard designs which make everything from outboard motors for boats to toasters to automobiles 'look'

4. London, B., *Ending the Depression Through Planned Obsolescence*. 1932. Pg 1-2.

functional while being anonymous enough not to attract too much attachment. Industrial design made replacement and 'upgrades' more important than repairing things for persistent use. By the 1960s, you were what you smoked, the house in which you lived, the car you drove, the synthetic fiber you wore, and modern advertising to this day continues the addiction.

The first cell phone was commercially produced in 1983. A decade later, cool businessmen, businesswomen, and doctors still had pagers and found payphones to be seen as urgently important. By the late 1990s, some of us had Motorola bricks and Palm Pilots. Smartphones are less than 20 years old but the likelihood is high that you've had dangerously close to as many phones as there have been years since they were released. Samsung, Apple, Nokia, Blackberry (...who?, oh the company that started the addiction)—been there, done that. And when Apple releases the iPhone 11, did anyone actually find the iPhone 10 so goddamn inadequate that they had to replace it? Nope. It's about the insignia of status. If you have an iPhone 11 in 2019, you have it because you have given me my segue to my next point.

While Brooks Stevens gave us the addiction to buy stuff in 1954 and built the media industry's obsession with advertising identity-based acquisition, somewhere around 1978, we were formally identifying the difference between brand preference or inertia and brand loyalty.[5] This distinction is important as the former says, "I bought a Ford because my dad bought a Ford," or "Nobody got fired for buying Big Blue," referring to IBM. The latter more significantly states that I am ceding to a brand a definition of what I need and who I am. Magazines, newspapers, billboards, commercials, pop-up ads, and the like all serve to remind you that you're depressed—there's a drug for that; you're too fat—don't wear stripes; you're a light sleeper—here's the mattress (oh, and a drug); you're too stressed—here's a vacation (oh, and a drug). How many food allergies, behavior disorders, health concerns, identity crises are manufac-

---

5. Jacoby, Jacob and Robert W. Chestnut., *Brand Loyalty: Measurement and Management.* (1978).

tured so that you identify with and consume the antidote for the thing you are or have?

For every planned obsolescence product of the 1950s, we were creating a persistent dependence on surrogated identity. What we consumed was meant to define who we were in social circles and to confirm our status. We were herded into consumption corrals and force-fed what we were told would validate our existence. Not only were we defined by what we consumed, we were dictated what we were, what consumption was either the badge or cure of that identity, and then coached, counseled or coerced into frenetically keeping up with whatever is the latest fad. Don't think for a moment that your 5-year-old you would eat kale (oh, there you go again, Dave)! You hated spinach and kale is spinach with sharp edges!

Pointless editor's note: *If you're reading this book and you have a cell phone with a flat screen, you've done more to contribute to global warming than the average human in the past 100 years. What I mean by that is that our consumption behavior is responsible for most of what's screwing up our environment. Copper mining genocide, rare-earth metals torture and rape, lithium battery lung disease, and factory toxins to numerous to count all so you can have your device du jour. So, don't Tweet about the environment on your smart phone. The giant caterpillar in the sky is watching you and you'll lose your wings!*

When what you consume as a definition of identity fully takes root, a more interesting consumption emerges—narratives. While Twitter took it to the 128 character extreme (limiting to a few lines, the conveyance of a thought), the 'stuff consumption' identity was delivered in small temporal intervals defined by the TV and radio commercial, the dimensions of ads, and the occasional gadget 'conference' for the great unveiling of next season's whatever. From the Detroit auto show to COMDEX to the laser light show productions for Tesla and Apple, what you never knew you needed was debuted with such fanfare that, while you may have normally been scratching your head going, "why do I need three cameras on my phone," the frenetic nature of the messenger blinded you to the pointlessness of the 'need'.

In 1836, Parisian media personality Emile de Girardin introduced paid advertisements to reduce the cost of *Le Presse*. It took four years for the innovation to get across the pond and in 1840, Volney Palmer set up America's first advertising agency with his innovation of buying space in newspapers and then reselling the space to clients seeking to promote whatever they were hawking. Palmer and de Girardin's introduction of advertising into the 'news' was an important social transformation. What constituted 'news' not only got blurred with the placement of paid promotions, but the shape of editorial content began to be influenced by advertiser influence. And while indoctrination was once the province of religious and political orders, implicit indoctrination became ubiquitous throughout media. 'Real' was that which was sponsored and curated.

Ask anyone today about political party affiliation and you're likely in for a wild diatribe about sides. Old school indoctrination around right and wrong and 'us' and 'them' has not—as our TV human emergence evangelists suggest—given way to more thoughtful engagement and understanding. The constant influence of ever more diffuse exposure to ad content, now a constant feature in all of our primary modes of communication, has shaped our thoughts, values, and actions in ways that defy metrics. Emotional and physical health news is an infomercial for the latest intervention. Style and design dictate the irrelevance of anyone who steps away from the consume-extinguish-replace merry-go-round.

And potentially one of our greatest destructive forces is *the consumption of sanctioned narratives of victimhood*. During the writing of this book, I experienced the destruction of a career of one, and the suicide of another, acquaintance all born of the consumption of the dominant theme of the open warfare between men and women. The drumbeat of public disclosures of horrific violence perpetrated by some men on some women has occupied the media with incessant fascination. I fully endorse the public action to end the scourge of male-perpetrated violence. From the rape culture from university fraternities, to the reprehensible practice of pedophilic marriage practices in regions of Africa, India, and the Middle East, we must bring abuses to an end. But absent from this conversation is the socially neglected cruelty endorsed by women for women on men.

The career that ended above came from a female student in a classroom seeing pictures of clouds that looked like, and are named for breasts, and reporting the science teacher as a harasser. The suicide referenced above came from a husband of over 30 years recognizing that his only socially acceptable option to deal with an emotionally intolerable marriage was to end is life. The widow's response? More should be done about men's mental health.

Here's a little public service announcement for women reading this book. Good men who kill themselves as their last act of honor *are not suffering from mental health issues*. They're suffering from sociopathic conditions born of untenable social stigma. To stand up to the woman who has abdicated her participation in a partnership in favor of 'taking care of children'; become indifferent to sexual engagement, projects presumed social clichés of 'looking at other women' because 'all men do it' regardless of manifestly evident fidelity; and, countless other tyrannies, many men find that living with the shame of admitting the end of socially sanctioned incarceration is worse *than ending their lives*. You can't watch a female comedian without seeing crowds of women wildly applauding that with marriage, sex can finally be ignored. "Get your man," is funny… only for women. And when decades on, the pain of indifference, the use of pornography, the constant fidelity for no obvious reason piles shame upon shame, men are left with no means of escape.

The fact that men are 3.5 times more likely than women to kill themselves is *not a mystery*. And the fact that this number is growing far worse in a peculiar tandem to the #MeToo movement is entirely ignored. I know, from personal experience, the pain of going for long bicycle rides in the country roads of Virginia and looking at where downhills and bends in roads would lead investigators to conclude that I had "lost control of my bike" so that ending my life wouldn't rob my family of life insurance windfalls. A mental health problem? Far from it. It was the ending consequence of what Gregory Bateson describes as a double bind. You observe a condition that cannot be altered. You see an unambiguous way to address the situation. You convey your pain to a person you love who says they love you back. And their response? Do nothing! So, as a final act of service to that person, you conclude that removing your life from the equation ends your pain and gives them the ability to live without you as a distraction!

While I'm in no way suggesting that #MeToo should be diminished, I am explicitly stating that the consumption of that social meme is going to place more men in positions where *by virtue of being men*, they can be targeted by adolescent students in classrooms and indifferent decades-married wives as 'being the problem' with no regard for the damage that this behavior unleashes. I'd suggest that the majority of people who are mystified by the fact that 70% of the 22 suicides per 100,000 people are men between the ages of 45-64 *are women who don't give a shit.*

In the past 40 years, I've had the great fortune of working with hundreds of women recovering from sexual abuse, neglect, and violence. I've seen the pain that persists from childhood to old age from abuses of all sorts. I've worked with many men who were victims of clerical abuses within churches and soldiers indelibly marked by the carnage of war. I've worked with the survivors of genocide on three continents and have brought tools of constructive reengagement to thousands. I've worked with innumerable men and women who have been exposed to the very worst of humanity. My own body bears scars of my own experience with unimaginable torture and cruelty. In my own life and in the lives with whom I've worked, I've worked to avoid the consumption of victim narratives. And I say 'consumption' because this, in my estimation, is the worst thing to take in.

What we do with the experiences of our lives is ultimately a decision. We can see the events in life as a vast conspiracy of occult forces arrayed for our demise. Or we can see the events as just that. Events. Christian insanity notwithstanding, Roman crucifixion is *not divine love and sacrifice*. It's murder—pure and simple. Comedic indifference towards married men is not funny. It's socially sanctioned emasculation and cruelty. These are, albeit regrettable, just events. When we define ourselves with the victim narrative of the same, we *add our own life force and obsession to that which has no place in humanity*. It doesn't deserve more energy.

In contrast, we can examine the motivations for behaviors. We can see the series of expedient compromises that lead to metastatic, destructive abuses. Rather than allowing ourselves to enter into the pattern of the tyranny born of the accumulation of tiny expediencies, we can observe reflexive social patterning and interrupt its attachment in our life. If you care about genocide, don't buy a phone from a company that refuses to disclose the source of their metals. If you don't want to contribute to the premature deaths of lithium miners—don't buy a Tesla. If you don't want to see men die at their own hands from relationship-induced futility, don't laugh about the cessation of sexuality when female comedians make it the punchline of jokes. A better humanity is born from a humanity that is thoughtful, considered, and respectful—and capable of critiquing uncomfortable topics without dismissing them!

For the past 90 years—which means only a select few of us have a dim recollection—we've been trained to be voracious caterpillars indiscriminately chewing up the fodder we've been fed about obsolescence. The resulting pestilence on the land, water and air is already choking our masticating muscles. No wings for you! No transcendence on the horizon. Just a giant pizza eating, gooey sac! As long as your identity is defined or informed by your consumption you are incapable of accessing *your essence*.

X

'Why' Are You Here?

his is the chapter that I care about the most. It's the hardest to write and will likely be the most challenging to read and assimilate. That's due, in part, to the fact that I've seen countless lives lost—both real and figurative—by people who are on a stage not of their selection, playing out roles that they were assigned but did not choose, and finding in both the stage and the actors a story that ends in tragedy or suffering in this life and too often trading it for an illusion of a better 'next'.

I've seen individuals, relationships, communities, countries, and civilizations incapable of fulfilling their potential based largely on the 'belief' that they're helpless in altering the manner in which they think. Possibly worst of all, I see the cunning social technology that was invented to domesticate and enslave the human potential and I'd love to see that dynamic altered. That technology, likely refined by Aristotle in the 4th century BCE, was the invention of *WHY*.

We don't have modern writings or philosophies that don't include the cunning tool of causality to enslave the mind. And while we can read Aristotle's writings (as they've been translated) and attribute 'why' and 'causality' to him, we don't know if he is the author he's credited to be. What is clear is that with the invention of 'why', we constrained life and our world to things that we think we know and *predicted, future uncertainties*. With this invention in Greek-influenced 'civilization', we lost our capacity to do many of the things that persist in megalithic artifacts that show a humanity less constrained. When we seek to reduce the beautifully entangled universe to x-y plots of data through which we draw lines to explain 'why' and 'what's next' we exclude variables (energy, matter, and perspectives) that don't fit on graphs. So, in the chapter that follows, I'm going to do my very best to help you unlock the shackles of causality, the blinders of 'knowing', and emancipate you to living *your life* with neither meaning nor justification. That's right, I simply would like you to—using my wife Kim's mantra—*Fully Live!*

A tiny note of encouragement here, dear reader: this section gets slightly complex but, courage! You have not stretched some of the muscles that you have and, sometimes exercising thoughts that have been atrophied takes a bit of stretching so, do a little yoga, stretch your quads and hammies, and let's get on with it. It's worth getting this so that we can get to the good bits at the end. It would be lovely to make an agreement here. Please read this slowly. Frequently stop (or at least slow down to sloth speed) and let a sentence or paragraph sit and marinate. If something doesn't make sense, back up and take another shot. You'll get it!

> *Life's but a walking shadow, a poor player*
> *That struts and frets his hour upon the stage*
> *And then is heard no more: it is a tale*
> *Told by an idiot, full of sound and fury,*
> *Signifying nothing.*[1]

Well, that's a damn depressing way to start a chapter! Here's a thought. Read it aloud with your best British accent. There, doesn't it sound better? OK, you're not going to make the London stage. But seriously, 'why' are you here? In the preceding chapters we've seen that much of the world we think we understand and the identity that we've taken on has been served *to* us to form us into something or someone. But we're not entirely sure who's behind this. What's the point (or their point)? By placing in the hands of someone or something our life and its energy, we seek to know that we're doing the right thing, making a difference, being relevant. Life's got to have meaning, right? *By*

---

1. Shakespeare. *The Tragedy of Macbeth*. Act V, Scene 5. 1607.

obsessing about 'mattering', we've made ourselves and our lives irrelevant.

Let's take this one piece at a time. We're going to start with the creation myth of causality—that things exist and happen for a 'reason'. We were taught this. It's not part of our biologic operating system—it's a software program that's loaded through our 'civilization' or, more appropriately our 'domestication'. From there, we'll examine the math that indoctrinates our view that the 'future' can be 'predicted' from the 'past'. And after examining that little gem, we'll take on the heroin of 'hope'.

Causality is a philosophical abstraction derived from our unwelcome friend, 'belief'. While we're guessing through a lens shaped by our current notions, Aristotle is credited with introducing the notion of 'cause' as a means of *explaining a phenomenon*. That which 'is' happens. But for a host of motivations, we're habituated into a notion that 'is' fits into a bigger narrative that has motivation. In Book II of Aristotle's *Physics* he suggests that nature simply exists. When things are manipulated in nature—like the shaping of stone, the cutting of wood for furniture or fuel, etc—these purposes build a narrative organizing a sequence of steps explaining a phenomenon. Why was the wood cut? For the fire. Why was the stone carved? Because someone wanted to imprint a symbol or message.

> *"Knowledge is the object of our inquiry, and men do not think they know a thing till they have grasped the 'why' of it (which is to grasp its primary cause)."*[2]

STOP! Just let that one settle in. We don't 'know' something without knowing the motivation behind it? That's BS! And shortly, I'm going to demonstrate that the way we view a set of facts tells multiple stories based on *our observation perspective* not based on the 'is-ness' of the facts.

Underpinning Aristotle's inquiry was a Greek legal principle of accountability.[3] Who's responsible? What's responsible? Who's to blame or credit? All of these questions are born of our cultural propensity to think,

---

2. Aristotle. *Physics: Book II*. §3. Circa 350 BCE.
3. The Greek term is *'aition'*.

or seek to make sense, of things. And 'to *make* sense' we must take what we actually *sense* (from the observations and inputs in our environment) and formulate them into a story that includes pieces that we *do not sense* at the same time. A few pages ago (in Chapter IX), I said we'd get to this again and, lucky for both of us, I remembered to fulfill my promise. The world is happening. We're part of the world. At any point, we're stimulated by things that elicit perception. These, as I suggested before, are merely awareness. To formulate an idea, we put these perceptions into our cognition like push-pins in the gooey map of other experience in our brain and color in the space demarcated by the pins. This formulation of 'an idea' makes sense of the inputs. Then, to this abstraction, we build a story on either side of it to 'understand' the motivations of, or causes for, that which we observed.

Pause for a moment. Let's walk into our garden on a summer morning. We see a crawly green phytophage on a leaf (remember our cool name for caterpillars?). It's eating the kale that we have dutifully planted for our yummy salad. We've been told that, for heart health, for post-modern 'cool points' and trendiness, we must eat kale. While we're watching, a white butterfly lands on a kale plant and deposits eggs. So far, just facts. We're just observing what's going on without putting 'meaning' on it. What happens next? With the same set of facts we can construct several "meaning" stories.

- <u>Story 1</u>: *Thank god the caterpillar's eating that stuff so I don't have to.* This story is born of a narrative of finitude, scarcity and competition. Whatever the caterpillar eats, I don't have to because it will be gone. There's only a limited supply and its either me or the caterpillar.

- <u>Story 2</u>: *Nature is out to get me because god sent a caterpillar to eat my heart disease-preventing kale so I'm going to die.* This story is born of conspiratorial cosmology and fate. Somehow the universe is conspiring for or against my well-being and existence. It was just 'meant' (by some deity or order) to be!

- **<u>Story 3</u>:** *While I was planning on eating the kale, I'm glad the butterflies have found a place to live and thrive.* This story means that you're a city dweller who has never fought off pests on your garden, dammit! *Ooops, sorry about that outburst.* This one means that you see your capacity to apply effort to the betterment of the ecosystem and your caloric (and cool points) 'needs' are interchangeable with the satisfaction of inter-species symbiosis. In other words, you don't really give a shit but making up a story that feels good is making you feel good. You probably also recycle plastic bottles to 'help the environment' without considering that the environment would have been much better off without you buying the plastic bottle in the first place. But, hey, you're doing your part, right?

Are you getting the point? Our pursuit of explanations and rationalizations is entirely capricious and shaped by our emotions, our worldview, the previous events in our day, to name a few. We have a hard time just observing and letting the observation simply be. Maybe a phytophagous caterpillar is eating kale. Maybe neither it, nor you, entirely know why. After all, it's kale so maybe neither of you really like it, but it's just there, and eating is happening. Now I'm using this comic set of examples to help you reflect on the 'whys' that you've asked today, yesterday, a week ago or throughout your life. And it would be nice if you pause, remove the comedy of the caterpillar and see if you can see *most of your 'whys'* somewhere in these three examples.

Now that we've entered into questioning the question a bit, let's go deeper.

There must be a 'because'. Like 'why', 'because' serves to allow us to adjudicate morals and values upon the lived experience. Seeking to justify the suitability or lack thereof of a thing, circumstance, or behavior, we can formulate trajectories of value determining whether something is 'good' or 'bad'. The fact that each one of us takes on the role of judge, jury, and executioner on these numerous, often trivial, determinations

subtly reinforces a power complex in which we seek and impose dominion on others, events, and things. By imposing judgments *on* things,
we establish both our hierarchical position, and we also place a finality
around unconsidered other perspectives that may alter our view if we
were willing to leave things open-ended.

In the early summer of 2015, I spent a week away at a Buddhist
monastery in Colorado. Perched atop mountains near Durango, I was in
a tiny cabin alone with no other human contact. On the second morning
of my sojourn, I decided to give myself a challenge—spend an entire day
without words. By this, I didn't just mean silence. I meant interrupting the impulse to identify anything as the term that describes it. And I
meant, not thinking either. Just let the day unfold and participate in it
without any 'story'. The experience was exceptionally difficult…and one
of the most significant moments of my life.

I wrote the following the day after my fast from words:

> *I watched a small oak, a tall pine, wild grasses and prayer flags*
> *across the course of this day. The wind warned of its arrival with the*
> *rushing sound in distant trees reminding me of the flow of a broken*
> *wave. The blue, white, red, green, and yellow flags all seemed hun-*
> *gry for every breath of wind. None of the grasses moved in unison*
> *and, try as I might, I could not discern the variation. Height, weight*
> *of seed and pollen, proximity of leaves; none seemed to dictate in*
> *the moment how the grass would move. The oak leaves shook with*
> *ecstasy in many of the gusts twisting their stems in a frenzied whirl.*
> *The pine needles didn't appear to move at all but, with the gust, the*
> *branches oscillated in a slower rhythm made more notable by the*
> *exuberant shudders of the oak below.*
>
> *As I watched this dance, I was brought to a series of inquiries.*
> *As one considers the geometry of the flag, the head of grass, the oak*
> *and the pine, what factors contribute to their divergent response to*
> *the same wind? The flags are cloth with tattered edges more like the*
> *pollen on the head of grass. Twenty-five seed heads stagger them-*

selves up the stalk; each kernel shrouded with six husks. The pollen filaments hold two or three delicate yellow tendrils bound to the grain by nearly imperceptible silk threads. The oak with its seven prominences is not symmetrical. Nineteen major veins launch from the stem and each form the base of a lattice of ever smaller capillaries reaching into each cluster of cells containing groups of 5 to 8 walls. The pine has crowns of 36 sets of three needles—each needle of nearly the same diameter and length. Homogeneity, it seems, moves the whole without greatly impacting the individual. Heterogeneity quakes the individual but has subtle effects on the whole. I wonder if the symmetry of the grains and pine contribute to their fast growth but weak fiber while the cacophonous shuddering of the oak leaf creates the oscillation that makes the oak hard.

I'm sorry that I've not stopped until today to ponder the nature of wind on nature. Its presence is variable. Its effect is variable. And the role it plays on life is evidenced in the bare felled trees with their twisted or straight fibers. The same light shines on them; the same soil nourishes them; the same wind caresses them and their response is the union of form and perspective. This union of form and perspective informs what Thomas Merton described, "a keen awareness of the interdependence of all things which are all part of one another and all involved in one another." And while Merton limited his thoughts towards what he called "living things", I am fascinated by any perspective that would not see the wind breathe, waves pulse, and grasses dance. Water, to evidence the fluid state of matter need not ebb and flow, yet it does. The seed that holds in it the propagation of next season's life or this season's food need not bow and straighten, yet it does. So, what then is life if it's not that ever-flowing present in which form and energy choose, in their ap-proximation, to act and interact?

Twenty-four hours of silence in both word and thought and suddenly, I was perceiving things that I had never considered. You'll notice that

I observed patterns and associations. I took those and reflected on other things that were not immediately present in my observation. But at no point did I answer any question. In fact, new inquiries were born of not asking why!

In his allegory of the cave, Plato posits that the rank and file of humanity (in his metaphor, chained to a wall observing dancing shadows cast by firelight on the cave wall) prefers inferring dimly through consensus stories and judgements rather than seeing the puppeteers, the fire by which their shadows dance, or god forbid, escaping the cave altogether and experiencing life on the surface in the sun. There are three consensus elements in his allegory: A fire; dancers and puppeteers behind a wall to which observers are chained on its opposite side; and the cave wall upon which the shadows are projected. This sequence can be represented in the first math you learned in algebra. The light from the fire is variable x. The dancers and puppeteers are the dynamic unknowns or b. Alternatively, we can substitute the fire or the dancers if we think one is variable and one is constant. And the shadows cast on the wall are the effects of our outcomes or y. Stated as a simple equation: if dancers perform between the source of light and the dark cave wall, will their shadows be seen on the wall?

When you were in math class—algebra most likely—you remember drawing x-axis (the base) and y-axis (the upright piece) graphs into which you put data points, lines or symbols. Like this:

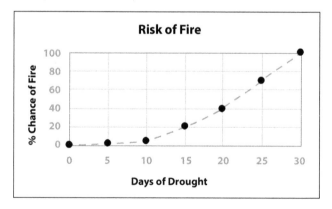

You were taught to put the independent variable (the thing you can measure in scale) on the *x* axis and the dependent or predicted variable on the *y* axis. Without telling you the rationale for it, you were then told to draw a line through the data points and calculate the slope of the line (which for the geeks reading this book is 3.364). You probably never knew what the point was, but you did it for your math test. You may remember the equation for calculating a predicted outcome:

$$y = mx + b$$

Now please calm down. I know you don't like math. You hated your algebra teacher. You were too busy passing notes to your boyfriend or girlfriend this day and, *because* of that, you flunked math and *because* of that you didn't become the doctor you wanted to be. And *because* of that, your parents are forever disappointed in you. And *because* of that, you had to get a shitty job waiting tables at a truck stop. And that's where you met Phil. And, well you know about Phil. He got mauled by a saber-toothed tiger. Whatever! This is *not a math lesson—it's a life lesson*.

We want to predict or know *y*. What's going to happen? To calculate *y*, we decided to measure something that we think we know *x* and something about its scale *m* (how much, how often, etc). To that we add unexplained variance or the 'shit-happens' error *b*. Put another way, the *b* is the socially accepted assumption that serves as the narrative around causation. It's never measured, only ever assumed. And before long we ask…

- Why (*y*) did John die from lung cancer? Oh, didn't you know that John smoked 12 packs of cigarettes (*mx*) a day? Unspoken in this is the 'shit-happens' error *b* that *smoking* causes *cancer*. I'm not suggesting that smoke exposure may very well alter cells in a manner that is consistent with changes that manifest as cancer but not *all smoking* leads to *all cancer*.

- Why (*y*) did Amy die at only 9 years old? Didn't you know that heaven needed more angels (*mx*)? Unspoken in this is the 'shit-happens' error *b* that god capriciously gives and takes lives.

- Why (*y*) does my husband not want to have sex with me anymore? Didn't you know that he likes skinny girls (*mx*)? Unspoken in this is the 'shit-happens' error *b* that sexual attraction is dependent on weight.

- Why (*y*) do bad things happen to good people? Didn't you know that suffering in sufficient volume (*mx*) refines character? Unspoken in this is the 'shit-happens' error *b* that things are distributed based on some sort of meritocracy (and that bad things don't happen to bad people).

- Why (*y*) is my life feeling like it's aimless and meaningless? Don't you know that it takes more time (*mx*) for your real purpose to emerge? Unspoken in this is the 'shit-happens' error *b* that it's time and not your recalcitrance to unaltering perspectives or objections to the present that precludes you from engaging meaningfully today.

Try as you might, the likelihood that you'll find out why we use *y* to explain why is elusive. But there's a pretty good guess when looking at who appears to have introduced it into common use. Gottfried Leibniz wrote his dissertation entitled *A Metaphysical Disputation on the Principle of Individuation* in 1663. He suggested that analytic philosophy needed to be explained through mathematics and, lo and behold, he's the guy (or at least one of the guys) that came up with the notation *y* for why! With 26 letters from which to choose (actually a few more variants in German), he went with *y*!

Leibniz attempted to build a logical bridge between the observed world and the prevailing Christian nostalgia of his time. As a philosophical theist—partially arising from the conflict of being baptized Lutheran but a beneficiary of wealthy Catholics—he sought to bring mathematical objectivity to the Sacraments and mysteries of religion. And by suggesting that the world was compartmentalized into individual pieces he predicated his work on explaining events that unfold when perceived through separation. In other words, cause and effect.

As we habituate 'why', we begin to define ourselves by our stories of ourselves. We are variously heroes or villains, winners or losers, princes or paupers based on the degree to which we think we're controlling or being controlled by the choreography of the events of our lives. Events don't just happen. They must have *meaning*. After all, what's the point if life simply unfolds? By the time you… well, if you're reading this… you are hard-pressed to know whether you actually know who you are in contrast to the carefully curated story of who you say you are derived from your causal narrative.

- "I'm miserable now (y) because I was abused as a child ($mx + b$)."

- "I'm comfortable in my life now (y) because my wife and kids love me ($mx + b$)."

- "I'm sick now (y) because I didn't exercise enough when I was younger ($mx + b$)."

Do you notice the pattern in these? We reduce the quantum entanglement of the ever-present-unfolding-now and decide that an outcome is derived from one or a few actions that we judge to be either good or bad based entirely on our expectations. We try to put the infinitely-influenced-now on a graph paper and draw a line. But we don't know the variables despite our certainty that we must. Like the *Butterfly Effect* at the beginning of the book, we carelessly conclude causality when there is no evidence whatsoever that any of the variables are even associated with one another. We try to hold onto the pieces of 'evidence' that tell us that our formula works, and we lose sleep, lose relationships, become depressed, kill ourselves, and congratulate our fortune when they either work or not.

Back to the graph above for a moment. Have you ever puzzled over the unusual tendency that we have to draw graphs with just the field to the upper right of the *x-y* axis? This is *not by accident*. We want to see a world where 'things get better'. Whether its years of work and our pay (which should go up); years of marriage and our partner's accommodation of our shit (which should go up); days we keep our New Year's resolutions and our general hotness (which should go up), we inhabit a social conception that life happens in the 'improving future'. This is the way things *should be*. 'Should' is a prediction.

- "I did everything right so things should have worked out."

- "I gave my tithe at church or my charity to the homeless so I should have gotten 'blessed'."

- "I ate right, didn't drink or smoke, exercised so I should have been able to avoid heart disease."

- "I prayed so my sorrow should end."

Do you see the formula playing out in nearly all our worldview? We plot our observations of the now and then draw the line up and right to where we want the line to go. Never knowing whether any of the 'whats' are the right levers to pull, we pull on them and expect a beneficial outcome. And when it doesn't work, it's never our 'fault'. We have an excuse—someone or something messed things up. Thank god we have someone to blame. And it gets more pervasive.

"I hope."

Back in Chapter I we talked about hope. You remember, the notion that things which are suboptimal now get better or that a negative outcome is our 'next'? Hope lives in the upper right quadrant. Better. Than what? We're not sure but we're sure that we want 'better'.

In addition to the delusion of placing the events of our lives and our purpose on a stage not of our making and as an actor not of our casting, we embody a propensity to simplify life into predictable patterns of success or failure—things working out for or conspiring against us—and we begin to keep track of how often we get the story 'right' (confirming our predictions) and 'wrong' (something's out to get us).

Please re-read this preceding paragraph because it's SUPER important.

Rather than taking on accountability for how we show up, we find ways to make it about others, about circumstances, about cosmic forces, about fate. *These are all illusions.* Wonder what's making relationships challenging, life exhausting, and effort feel pointless? Consider the amount of time you 'try to make sense' of what's just happened. And then add to that the complexity of trying to convince others that they should be part of your illusions or delusions. How many arguments, disagreements, conflicts or open hostilities arise from people insisting that they 'know' the motivations for, and intents of the actions of others?

Rather than 'making sense' of life, could we consider living? By this I mean the practice of commencing each day with gratitude for the fact of our existence—the fact of the sun's light, the fact of our shelter, our nourishment of body and emotions, our beating heart, our breathing lungs, our alchemical mitochondria—and then the living of each day with reverence and elegance. Or have we fallen for possibly the most insidious social platitude of modernity—the *Golden Rule.*

I despise the *Golden Rule* and all of its corollaries for the same reason I despise 'why'.

"Do unto others as you would have them do unto you."

This crock of shit has justified a transactional morality and is ubiquitous across nearly every religious catechism. I call this 'transactional morality' as it uses the predicted receipt of treatment as the standard for that which you should strive to effect. People lose their minds when someone or something 'disappoints' them (fails to conform to their $y = mx + b$ illusion), leaves them in the lurch, or doesn't deliver expected behaviors or results. "How could they...?" WTF? The institution of transactional morality means that you run around the world with expectations (the predicted outcomes from the set of variables you decide are important) and when the world doesn't revolve around you, you get pissed. Well, *News Flash*! The world doesn't revolve around you. Because *you are not the (a) point.* You are a temporary arrangement of matter and energy that is inextricably part of the fabric of everything and as such, your mission, should you choose to accept it, is to make your best contribution regard-less of the challenges, the frustrations, the pains or the joys. Do not unto, but with others. As elegantly as possible—not to someone else's standard. And celebrate the propagation of your goodness and elegance rather than expecting it to bounce back to you. Far from the *Golden Rule*—this is the *Lightness of Life!*

XI

Who the Hell Are YOU?

✦❧✦

George Bernard Shaw wrote:

> *This is the true joy in life, being used for a purpose recognized
> by yourself as a mighty one. Being a force of nature instead of
> a feverish, selfish little clod of ailments and grievances, com-
> plaining that the world will not devote itself to making you
> happy. I am of the opinion that my life belongs to the whole
> community and as long as I live, it is my privilege to do for it
> what I can. I want to be thoroughly used up when I die, for
> the harder work, the more I live. I rejoice in life for its own
> sake. Life is no brief candle to me. It is a sort of splendid torch
> which I have got hold of for the moment and I want to make
> it burn as brightly as possible before handing it on to future
> generations.*[1]

This quote seems to be a great place to start this final Chapter on examining who you are, who I am, and who we are as a whole community.
And the good news for you is I'm not going to answer the question about
you. That's yours.

But I'll do my best to give you a picture of who I am and, with any
luck, from the way I lay it out, you may take some time and reflect on
how you'd tell your story if it was just that—YOURS!

Before I go any further, it might be helpful to briefly introduce a per-
spective-shaping tool I use call Integral Accounting. I use this technique

---

1. George Bernard Shaw. *Man and Superman*: Epistle Dedicatory. Pg. xxxii. 1903.

to examine *everything* through six dimensions or perspectives. In so doing I can more carefully examine a thing (person, situation, object) and be more completely informed. The six dimensions or perspectives are:

<u>Commodity</u>: simply the matter and energy of the Universe

<u>Custom and Culture</u>: the appearance of matter and energy in observable dimensions and the consensus on what is observable

<u>Knowledge</u>: the transmittable experiences and stories arising from observation, interaction, and contemplation

<u>Value / Money</u>: the hierarchy or priority that sets one thing above another in importance

<u>Technology</u>: the agencies whereby we manifest consensus experiences in repeatable manner

<u>Well-being</u>: the optimal performance of a thing at liberty in its most unconstrained form

To view these perspectives, I like to use guiding questions that assist in elucidating the essence of my actual experience—not the selective narrative informed in a particular emotional or temporal observation. Each perspective defined above is discerned through the following set of inquiries:

1. What are the 6 places or things that most significantly imprinted on or impacted your life?

2. Who are the 6 people and community experiences that most shaped or influenced your life?

3. What 6 things do you *know to be true* from your lived experience?

4. What 6 things do you value most—both things that helped and harmed you the most?

5. What 6 behaviors or practices do you most frequently and consistently engage?

6. What are your 6 greatest accomplishments or disappointments?

I was born in a massive blizzard in North Dakota and spent my early childhood in Southern California surrounded by oceans, mountains, deserts, lakes and rivers. With a father who was an astronomy teacher and researcher, I was exposed to people deeply fascinated in globular clusters, galaxies, super nova, etc. With a mother trained as a linguist, I observed the supreme power of human nature incarnating untold forces of good and evil through the use and manipulation of language. Albeit through the lens of religion, the manifest power of nature in all of its forms was the most significant imprint in my life.

My community experiences had to do with transient love, affection, and engagement. From my early experiences with death and murder to the fact that our family was extremely transient never living in a place for more than a few years at a time, family and community were temporary. Just about the time I'd feel connected to anyone, I'd lose them. Given the preeminent role of religion in my life, "love" was always a transactional notion. You were 'in' if you conformed, toed the line, and acquiesced to the merits of rejecting the present for an eternal 'better'. Fail to conform—you lose your family, your friends, your sense of belonging—to say nothing of the frequent physical punishment justified under the perverse notion that violence begets moral conformity. My experience of temporary (and in most cases, conditional) love had the effect of manifesting a longing for connection that I perceived to be the experience of others.

I always perceived a world without boundaries or limits. I lived in the tension of a world in which I was to "believe" in religious fantasies but was not allowed to have my own unsanctioned perceptions. I didn't know that my unconstrained perspectives were unusual early in life and, as I grew, marveled at the propensity I saw in others to build obstacles that kept them from fully living. My earliest memories involve an appreciation that I could connect to other things and sense with and through them. In short, I had the knowledge that everything was connected and that everything, in its native condition, was capable of perceiving, remembering, and teaching. I knew that the hybridization and domestication of humans through the agency of fiat conformity broke this connection and that uniquely, humans manufacture the illusions of mystery and contemplation to escape the self-evident, manifold wisdom that surrounds each moment if you merely perceive.

Genuine matters! Throughout my life, I find that those things that were most cherished in my life were moments, experiences, and interactions that were genuine. The contrived, the orchestrated, the fake and the manipulated all seem to suffer from the energies of seduction and manipulation and inevitably end in disappointment. My life is punctuated with the staccato of genuine people, moments, experiences and things against the monotonous drone of parasitic superficiality in which my utility to others far exceeds a notion of reciprocal or generative interaction. This serves to heighten my gratitude for the genuine moments when they arise.

Our present model of physics puzzles over what makes the photon activate for propagation of light just like our biochemistry models are impotent in explaining what gives rise to the pace-making electrical impulse of the heart. Because we seek to identify the 'source' or 'beginning', we struggle with the notion of activation without clear provocation. In nature, this happens. In my life, this happens. My life has been an effusive flow of energy in service to and consumed by others. That it persists, at times mystifies me (particularly when I'm feeling like I'm tapped out of energy), yet it continues to flow.

I receive great satisfaction from the recollections of contributions I've made throughout my life. The notion that many of my efforts have contributed to beneficial effects in personal, business, and civic settings is of considerable value. At the same time, some of my deepest disappointments have come from extensive effort applied to people or situations in which, despite my best intentions, benefit and outcomes either were not evident or, in certain instances, seemed to become more remote with my intervention. Whether it's the reforestation of the land where I make my home, the reconciliation of warring communities, or the insertion of transparency into purposefully obscure financial markets, I have seen my life making a discernable and positive difference.

Now, take a moment and let me stitch a concept together. The preceding 6 paragraphs are the synopsis of the answers I had to the 6 questions listed above, which themselves are derived from the 6 dimensions or perspectives summarized just prior to the questions. The dimensions can be summarized in my story of my life into simple statements of energetics, observations, and values: In short, I feel connected to the powerful energy of nature; my sense of love and connection as been transient; I sense an accountability to live within an interconnected wholeness of all things; I value that which is genuine; I'm wired to provision that with which I interact; and, I am fulfilled with a sense of effectiveness. And while this is a map of the 'who' I am in my story of myself, these attributes help define places where I'm prone to struggle in my interactions with others.

While I experience the power of nature, I'm sensitive to feeling powerless as a 'doormat' that can be taken advantage of.

While I experience transient love, I'm motivated to a persistence in love that sometimes fails to recognize limits.

While I see the world as entirely interconnected, I struggle with evidence of separation and the proclivity to divide.

While I cherish that which is genuine, I'm constantly encountering incredulity and inauthenticity.

While I love to provide for others, I've emasculated my capacity of receiving from others.

While I love to sense that I've been effective, I'm doggedly pursued by a sense of futility for that which I have not achieved.

These dynamics integrate into a *story I tell* which is a selectively curated story of my life. And, for the purposes of example alone, I'd like to show you how varied *my own story* is depending on the audience. I'm going to let you see the same artifact of my own life through two lenses—one that is my introspective account of life and the other is my 'official bio' that is the marketing piece about my life. I would strongly encourage you to take some time to do this exercise on yourself to see how you and your persona interact both in the mirror and the projector of your life.

If I'm being introspective and deeply personal, this is my autobiography:

From my earliest memory, I perceived a number of things that were not shared perception. Using terms that were metaphoric ("see", "hear", "sense") I was constantly told by my parents that I "lied" when I would say I "saw" something. "That's not possible," would be their refrain before delivering physical punishment. Using my available language, my attempts to communicate awareness didn't conform to a consensus experience of perceived reality and therefore, I was 'wrong'. I found more solace in thunderstorms, mountains and oceans than I did in human interactions. What I 'knew' to be my genuine experience was something I was told I couldn't know. In the perversion of religious dogma, I witnessed 'love' being demonstrated by punishment, separation ("be in but not of the world"), and an unquenchable longing and sense of the unattainable. From before my birth, my mother echoed the refrain that she had "given" her children to a higher power. But that higher power always seemed remote, capricious, and malevolent.

My first friend was killed in an avalanche. My best friend as a child was stabbed to death. My dad's father died in 1976. In each instance, I had a "knowing" of the death as it was happening—something that was never understood and served as the subject of great pain. When first I interacted with women, my awareness was precise to the pain that they'd experienced (many times from abusing men). Resolving not to be an abuser, I realized that my own physical desires must be suppressed so that I could effectively 'serve' the sanctuary benefit for those who were harmed. I was acutely aware of what others 'had' in both beautiful and horrible ways but my monastic resolve was to diminish my desires in service to others. Separated from my natural physical essence, I experienced the futility of the repeated interactions I had with women who were harmed by their own complicit actions or against their will. In 1985 when I met the woman to whom I would be married for nearly 30 years, during our first conversation, she forcefully stated that she would never love a man again. Rather than take that as a warning, I embraced the journey of being the love that she didn't know she was rejecting. During our relationship, we shared the honor of raising two children and influencing the lives of hundreds of others with our international efforts focused on providing housing to those who were in distress. Twenty-nine years of service later, on a summer day in New York City, she rejected the loyalty and fidelity that I manifested for years, choosing to embrace a path apart from that which I sought to build.

In business, social settings, and my deep personal work in service to others, the most common refrain I hear is some variant of "you're too good to be true," or "I can't believe that you've done all that you've done." While this is often stated in a benign complimentary incredulity, what follows is insidious. Because I don't engage with consensus methods in interactions, people presume that I am independently wealthy, purely altruistic, or devoid of any reciprocal desire. "It comes so easy for you," is a refrain that follows my life. As a result, while others benefit richly from my genuine generosity, I have had only a few interactions in my life where I can confidently state that I have experienced a balanced value exchange. Most tragically, this shows up in my experience of the most intimate of social interactions where my experience of love and friendship has most often been transactional, utilitarian, and transient to the point of me feeling disposable.

The greatest achievements I have had in my life are those that have been done largely in anonymity in the far-flung reaches of the world. The communities who have most directly benefited from my life and welcomed me—for days, months, or years—have included me as a member of their families, tribes, and groups. Those that have mounted the most vigorous opposition to my work have been political and financial institutions threatened by my actions and the knowledge I've revealed that doesn't support their agendas.

For 52 years of life, I have not frequently experienced joy or what most would call happiness. I have sought to make those experiences possible for others but I've not focused my kindness inwards. And like a man walking in the light for the first time after being imprisoned in a dark cell for decades, I am not sure how to navigate each element of that journey but I know that I'm taking my first, tentative steps.

If I'm marketing myself, this is my autobiography:

Dr. David E. Martin is the Founder and Chairman of M·CAM International, the global leader in innovation finance, trade, and intangible asset finance. He is the developer of the first innovation-based quantitative index of public equities and is the Managing Partner of the Purple Bridge Funds. He is the creator of the world's first quantitative public equity index—the CNBC IQ100 powered by M·CAM which is now reported by The Conference Board as U.S. and Global Leading Economic Indicators. He manages three Exchange Traded Funds. Actively engaged in global ethical economic development, Dr. Martin's work includes financial engineering and investment, public speaking, writing and providing financial advisory services to the majority of countries in the world. Dr. Martin is the architect and founder of the Global Innovation Commons and is the author of the international legal framework for the Heritable Knowledge Trust and Heritable Innovation Trust programs. He has pioneered global programs to bring corporate and stock market transparency to multi-national extractive industries and has been instrumental in repatriating value to countries which have been subject to corporate and financial abuses. His work on ethical engagement and stewardship of community and commons-based value interests is at the forefront of global financial innovation. Dr. Martin is a Batten Fellow at the University of Virginia's Darden Graduate School of Business Administration. He served as Chair of Economic Innovation for the UN-affiliated Intergovernmental Renewable Energy Organization and has served as an advisor to numerous Central Banks, global economic forums, the World Bank and International Finance Corporation, and national governments.

A spokesperson for global financial and intangible asset accountability and quality reform, Dr. Martin has worked closely with the United States Congress and numerous trade and financial regulatory agencies in the United

States, Europe, and Asia in advocating and deploying infrastructure to support growing reliance on contract and proprietary rights in business transactions. Under the leadership of Dr. Martin, M·CAM has supported the modernization of banking, intangible asset, tax, and accounting laws through its work with oversight agencies and policy makers.

Dr. Martin has founded several for-profit and not-for-profit companies and organizations and serves on several boards. In addition to his current business and social efforts, he was the founding Director of Melbourne's Centre of Applied Innovation. He served as Chairman and CEO of eSurface˚. He was the founding CEO of Mosaic Technologies, Inc., a company that developed and commercialized technologies in advanced computational linguistics, dynamic data compression and encryption, electrical field transmission, medical diagnostics, and stealth/anechoics. He was a founding member of Japan's Institute for Interface Science and Technology (IIST). He founded and served as Executive Director of the Charlottesville Venture Group. He has served as a board member for the Research Institute for Small and Emerging Business (Washington, D.C.), the Academy for Augmenting Grassroots Technological Innovations (India), the Charlottesville Regional Chamber of Commerce (Virginia), and the Charlottesville Industrial Development Agency (Virginia), Humanitad (U.K), Global Urban Development, and many other agencies dedicated to ethical human development. As international policy contributor, economist and futurist, Dr. Martin's work at The Arlington Institute (U.S.) included accurately forecasting the global financial crisis of 2008 and working with the launch of Singapore's Risk Assessment Horizon Scanning initiative.

Dr. Martin's work as a Fellow of the Batten Institute at the Darden Graduate School of Business Administration at the University of Virginia and his related work at the Indian Institute for Management Ahmedabad, India, has brought unprecedented curricular focus to areas of intangible-asset risk management, finance, and accounting standards. In addition to his academic work, Dr. Martin has closely advised innovation-based finance and investment programs in India, Bermuda, Brazil, China, Denmark, the

European Union, the United Kingdom, South Africa, the Islamic Republic of Iran, the United States, Mongolia, Egypt, Ecuador, Singapore, Germany, Slovenia, Vietnam, and the United Arab Emirates. He has served as the Constitutional and Economic advisor to the Autonomy Committee of East New Britain and New Ireland, Papua New Guinea and has worked with ethical trade frameworks for the Kingdom of Tonga, the Independent State of Samoa, Fiji, and Papua New Guinea.

*His work has been the subject of two internationally awarded documentaries, **Patent Wars** which highlights his work on reform of the global innovation system and **Future Dreaming: A Conversation with David Martin** which is a dialogue about humanity and its optimal interaction in the universe. He has spoken at the United Nations General Assembly on citizen-led peacemaking initiatives and has been featured on Bloomberg television and HBO's Last Week Tonight with John Oliver.*

A speaker, author, business executive and futurist, Dr. Martin's work has been engaged in every country on Earth. He works with his family in every endeavor of life. Together with his wife Kim, he directs the Breathing Enterprise and Fully Live workshops and facilitates implementation of Integral Accounting. Dr. Martin received his undergraduate (BA) from Goshen College, his Master of Science from Ball State University, and his Doctorate (PhD) from the University of Virginia.

To read the former is to see "*ME*" as a man who has experienced considerable pain in life. That's because, while in neither of my bios, I live with constant physical pain born of a life-altering accident in 1988. That experience—the loss of pain-free use of both of my legs—and its persistent effects has undoubtedly motivated my intensity to live. However, it has also probably motivated a rather insidious resentment for those who, without disability, seem to defer that which they're capable of. It's fascinating to read 'my own story' and see how much I don't include.

To read the latter is to also see "*ME*" though with far greater difficulty. The litany of artifacts of existence speak of a person who has had an improbable influence in even more improbable places. Notwithstanding all of those artifacts, one can only partially detect that which motivates my passion and that requires powers of observation that would not be readily accessed.

Ask me who I am right now and what I'd likely say that I'm a *Fulcrum Master*. Just to remind you, the fulcrum is the point around which a lever pivots or a spinning object maintains its stability and momentum. I, much to the chagrin of some, like to fiddle with those points when I see things working in ways that harm people, the environment or the collective consciousness. I carefully examine the inertial mass of systems, understand their persistence, and when I see what I determine to be dysfunction or harm, I seek to introduce a wobble that alters the course of whatever is harmful. More precisely, I've playfully called what I do a *Fulcrum Ninja* because many of my efforts to modify the leverage and inertia dynamics are done in stealth to limit opposition to my efforts.

Early in our relationship, Kim and I were going out in Gold Coast, Australia. Entering the elevator, we both observed a beautiful, tall, rugged-featured man smartly dressed and oozing *GQ* confidence. As I shrunk to the back of the elevator, it was abundantly clear that he was extremely attracted to Kim. When he exited the elevator, she pulled my arm sharply.

"Don't you ever do that again," she scolded in an unsympathetic tone.

I knew what "that" was but didn't want to address the issue.

"That guy was a good-looking man," I said seeking to redirect the conversation with a social platitude.

"You let me down by not standing confidently beside me and owning your space with me which meant he felt perfectly fine checking me out," she said bringing us back to the point.

Since my early teens, I viewed myself as more hobbit than Hercules. I had terrible acne and experienced the ever-present dynamic of those that 'looked nice' appearing to have a life far beyond my reach. While a reasonable athlete and remarkably fit, my accident at 20 meant that

I was going to be in a wheelchair, have innumerable surgeries, and live with a visible limp. More hobbit for me. One day after my first bilateral leg reconstructive surgeries, we went to a mall and, while wheeling down the corridor, a child was reprimanded by his sensitive mother for asking if I was a monster. I could see it! I had massive metallic braces on my legs, blood soaked surgical wraps, and was looking far from jovial. By 25, my hair was thinning. So, body image wise—I was no Adonis! And that image formed an identity that meant that, "I would never be with a beautiful woman," and that I was unattractive in my appearance.

Far from a moment of transformational emergence—beautiful butterfly moment—my life has been far more of the frequently molting, ever emerging shiny lizard. Each part of my life has been shaped by the jagged rocks of awareness that scrape away the 'skin' that no longer serves me. While I am still the organism that was, is and is to come, like the shedding of skin, I've had to face uncomfortable moments when, albeit in service to one phase of my life, I've got to let go of that which stands in the way of the *me* that is required in that moment.

So here we were in Gold Coast—I'm standing next to a very beautiful woman who has had the audacity to choose a life with me. I see a man who is—in my perspective—far more "attractive" than me and I shrink. Mystery? Not at all. Justifiable? Not at all. And the reason I'm sharing this story? Simple, for all of my life experience, for all of my perspectives and wisdom, I too am challenged to discontinue narratives that neither serve me or those around me. And maybe like you, I struggle with the fact that who I am has often been hidden behind stories that I tell myself derived from my perceptions of others' thoughts, statements, actions, or indifference. Unfortunately, my view of appearance was inextricably linked to access or exclusion. It was a credentialing to be "in" or "out".

But this struggle is not universal in our human experience. There are places where people not only are fully embodied in their own perception of themselves but actually adorn themselves to amplify energies, spirits, or attributes of their explicit connection to the greater whole in exaggerated ways. In Kokopo, East New Britain, I had the great fortune to have my appearance obsession challenged with the use of the term "mask". The previous day, while we were up in the mountains near the Komgi village meeting with the community elders, thunder rumbled on the peak just behind us as if on cue to punctuate salient points in our conversations. Having been interrupted with loud rolls of thunder for over 45 minutes, I finally stopped talking and paused. "What does the thunder mean in the Komgi tradition?" I asked.

Balsius responded, "The thunder is on that mountain when the spirits are walking through the forest to tell us to respect them. Some of them are faces that we know and some of them have faces that even we don't recognize but we must honor them," he explained. When he said, "Some of them *are* faces," I puzzled and asked if I had heard him correctly.

A more Western convention would be to say that they *have* faces. No, he really meant that the spirits are faces. Instantly my mind went to the wonderful carvings and objects that have fascinated so many which are referred to by outsiders as "masks". What did it mean that the spirits are faces, some known and some unknown? When I was in the Provincial Administrator's office, I asked our circle whether the term "mask" was ever used in the Baining or Komgi culture before outsiders came in.

I don't recall many moments where the depth of nostalgic sadness was quite so evident. "No," recounted one man, "we never called them masks and, as a matter of fact, we've always found that term offensive. In our custom, these faces are our way of identifying the spirits of the ancestors and the dreams of the future and they are very unique to a person and very unique to a situation." We went on to discuss that the faces and attire that are used in Custom (the Komgi word for ceremony) come from a spiritual interpretation of the energies of both the ancestors and the future manifesting themselves in, through, and on the temporal body of the wearer. Rather than "masking" or hiding an identity—an inextricable and, at times, nefarious connotation—these faces revealed the deeper spiritual identity of a person providing a means for people to gain

187

a more complete picture of the identity. Not only were these not masks, they were explicit projections of the dimensions of character that the naked body simply was inadequate to incarnate. The spirit face was an invitation to see a dimension beyond, not a means to conceal or subterfuge.

By cartooning the mask and allowing it to be a cultural artifact, ethnographers, artists, and cultural heritage connoisseurs entirely miss—and dishonor—what the spirit faces teach us. Namely, that the explicit invocation of the metaphysical realm through external symbols is an unalienable component of humanity and community which must be honored, celebrated and present in communal gatherings.

Who am I? Who are you? Who are we?

While you are not defined by others, if you are thoughtful and careful, you can get a good sense of who you are by the field effect you have. While you are not known "by the company you keep", you can know a lot by observing those you attract, those that are indifferent, and those you repel. Light and magnetism persist (meaning that they are in a continuous state), are generative (meaning that their influence on others is without preference, restriction, or need for validation), and are infinitely orthogonal (meaning that, regardless of perspective, the effect can be discerned). Like light and magnetism, you, as a inextricable part of nature, have effects that are persistent, are generative, and are perceived by others regardless of your comfortability with their observation.

I offered my reflections in the paragraphs above for three reasons. The first was to model a method for examining life to seek a deeper understanding of the overarching themes that animate existence. Using the 6 lenses of perspective informed by the six questions, it is easy to observe trends, patterns, and habits that help explain the responses that we have to life's unfolding. My second reason was to let you see that, regardless of what you think, how you feel, or your response, I think it's helpful to normalize the experience of sharing life—both its grit and glory—with each other thereby allowing us to more deeply understand one another. And finally, I did it to engage you in the dialogue born of our sojourn through this book. While I set out to convince you of nothing, I did seek to challenge assumptions in a way that would allow you to more clearly understand your core essence and then figure out how to engage with it in the broader community. You joined me on that journey and for that, I am deeply grateful.

At a monastery in Beijing on a very foggy night in 2004 I was sitting with a Confucian master. We were discussing his view of life as an endless flow of energies variously incarnating and then re-entering formlessness only to re-assemble at other moments. His face—shiny to near glowing—was bright in the firelight of the lamps in the garden.

"David," he looked at me intently, "I've seen the end of your life."

I found this comment paradoxical as we were discussing a timeless, beginning-less, endless existence.

"This is your last incarnation," he continued. "And in this incarnation—your gratitude incarnation—your life will end when you have ac-knowledged and thanked all of the beings, all the life-forces, and all the people who have helped refine you into the person you were meant to be. Your last act will come when you say 'Thank you' to the last energy that carried you through your lives."

I don't know all of the 'meaning' that lived within his insight. What I do know is that I'm deeply grateful for him and the lesson he taught me. You may be 'the one' who I didn't get to thank in person. And if you are, you read this sentence and, poof... I sublimate into pure light or keel over with a heart attack, well, thanks for the life, the insight, and the journey we've shared. I know I am grateful, and I would encourage you to pass that gratitude along!

Action

꙳

The lizard has often been overlooked; scholars who have noticed it tend to interpret it as either a decorative detail or a symbolic reference. My analysis of the evidence contained in literary and iconographic sources has brought me to a different conclusion: I believe the lizard appears not on account of its symbolic or decorative value but because such animals were kept by children as pets in antiquity. If the lizard is understood as a friendly beast rather than a sign of resurrection, the composition may be treated as a reflection upon childhood, human and divine, rather than an existential allegory.

—Jean Sorabella[1]

When the Romans buried children, it was not uncommon for them to mark the gravestones with the carvings of lizards. And while scholars have postulated various explanations for this practice, I rather like Jean's suggestion. Children at play in Roman courtyards were frequently reported to play with, and keep as pets, lizards.

I don't know about you, but the menagerie of beasts that Zach found in the backyard at our home in Virginia variously included crickets, turtles, snakes, cockroaches, lizards and all manner of creepy, crawly beasts. The one thing about lizards that makes them particularly fun is the pro-pensity to escape. So, if parents lost a child to an early death, it's not sur-prising that they'd 'find' a lizard that would hang around the memory of the deceased child. If I would have required memorializing Zach when he

---

1. *Eros and the Lizard: Children, Animals, and Roman Funerary Sculpture. Hesperia Supplements.* Vol. 41, Constructions of Childhood in Ancient Greece and Italy (2007), pp. 353-370.

was young, I can imagine that some sculpted vivarium of crawly things would have conveyed his essence far better than some sappy poem about an angel getting wings. In short, I suspect that the Romans had an idea about the *persistence of play* in the face of death.

I have a hunch that we gravitate towards butterfly analogies as a function of our not-so-subtle wish to be 'more beautiful' or 'more transcendent' than we feel we are. After all, what's not to love about watching the haphazard lyrical flight of a winged palate of exquisite color? But in addition to my objections to our obsession about the metaphor at the opening of this book, my far greater concern is the pathology of lottery winning odds that underpins our aspiration. Remember, the trinity of the flying goo sac? Eggs, larvae to chrysalis, and wings? Well, here's the bad news. Most eggs don't hatch. The ones that do rarely have sufficient food to eat their 54,000 pizzas to get ready to hang out in the chrysalis where many of them don't survive the elements, the birds, and curious kids with jars. And finally, on the day that the great unfurling of wings happen, most wings don't work and most cycles end. When we 'wait for our moment' to emerge as our beautiful, colorful, wafting-on-the-wind selves, *most of us don't make it*. And that's where voyeuristic inspiration is very damaging. When we celebrate the one butterfly that overcame the odds, we often do so in a room full of eggs and caterpillars that are simply not going to make it. We may be harming far more than we're helping with the metaphors we choose.

I don't know Oprah Winfrey. I know a small group of people who know her. I know a huge number of people who know somebody who knows her. What I perceive is that she is an exceptionally talented and motivated person who has attracted considerable followings. In a world which forced issues like race, sexual abuse and violence, teen pregnancy, alternative lifestyles, eating disorders into quarantined and hushed conversations, Oprah emancipated them – and many of her viewers – on daytime TV. Living an exceptionally public life, she has allowed millions of others to open up about topics that are usually relegated to discretion and secrecy. For that, I'm profoundly impressed. While she's been open to the voyeurism of millions looking in on her life, by association she may have enabled millions to think that her openness somehow translates into their lived experience. Like Eckhart Tolle, Deepak Chopra, Tony Robbins and others who trade on 'self-improvement' I wonder if by mass association, viewers and fans think they're vicariously living the thoughtful, challenging work that these individuals may very well be doing. And like I said in the section on discipleship, the danger we have is to reflect from our heroes and gurus that which makes them exceptional and set apart rather than seeing the light that emanates from and through them. Each of these – and countless others – dedicated to improving the lives of others have been abraded by the challenges of life. And it is their light persisting through these moments that is their greatness – not the celebrity projected upon them having emerged.

Having said this, I think that it's time that we get serious about what *Fully Living* truly is. The awareness and refining of our diverse and multifaceted senses; the equanimity of perception that can observe without passing judgment; the embracing of the ever unfolding present in which monotonous goodness characterizes most of our days; and, the constant opportunity before us to treat our lives and the lives and ecosystems with which we interact with reverence and elegance.

What if the world really counted on you? Live in it. Love it. And don't seek to fly away! We all need US!

Dr. David Martin, Founder and CEO of M·CAM, is what Buckminster Fuller described as "a verb, an evolutionary process — an integral function of Universe." An author, public speaker, business visionary, professor, oracle, researcher, father, and friend, David is a man Fully Living. He has served as a financial, business and government advisor in over 120 countries and has been featured for three decades in media and speaking around the world. From the starry expanses of Mongolia to the flashing lights of New York, his work is as passion-filled whether it's with a camel herder or a global CEO.

9 781735 011202